Colorado Volunteers in the Civil War

The New Mexico Campaign in 1862

Battleflag of the First Colorado Regiment.

(From a photograph of the flag, which is now in the War-relic Department of the Headquarters of the Grand Army of the Republic, Department of Colorado and Wyoming,
in the Capitol at Denver.)

The rents shown in the upper part of the engraving were made by Confederate grapeshot in
the second engagement in La Glorieta Pass, March 28, 1862. Major Jacob Downing, of
Denver, stated that the color-bearer was Sergeant William B. Moore, of his company
(D), who was promoted Second Lieutenant shortly after the battle.

Colorado Volunteers in the Civil War

The New Mexico Campaign in 1862

BY
William Clarke Whitford, D.D.
PRESIDENT OF MILTON COLLEGE

ILLUSTRATED

The Rio Grande Press, Inc.
GLORIETA, NEW MEXICO · 87535

New Material
© 1971 The Rio Grande Press, Inc.,
Glorieta, N. M.

First edition from which this edition was
reproduced was supplied by
INTERNATIONAL BOOKFINDERS, INC.,
P. O. Box 3003
Beverly Hills, Calif. 90212

A RIO GRANDE CLASSIC
First Published in 1906

LIBRARY OF CONGRESS CARD CATALOG
74-150964

ISBN 0-87380-171-7

1994

The Rio Grande Press, Inc.
GLORIETA, NEW MEXICO · 87535

When Valor Failed

Socorro, April 30th, 1862.

My Dear Wife:—Having an opportunity to do so, I write you a letter by James Davis, who leaves here today for home, and who will probably get there some months before I can, for if I can get work in this country, I think I had better stay until winter at least, when I hope this war will be over. Well, here I am, with fifty-two others, on our way south, all afoot, with but three wagons that have been furnished us by our enemies to go home with. When we will get there the Lord only knows. With what a different feeling we pass through these Mexican towns now, from what we did two months ago. Then we felt like heroes, having had a fight at Fort Craig, scaring the Mexicans to flight, and driving the regular soldiers into the Fort, and getting past with our whole army and cutting off all supplies and relief to the Fort; we were marching up the country with the fixed determination of wrenching this country from the United States Government and we all thought it would soon be in our hands. But what a mistake. Having marched to within eighty miles of Fort Union, we were again met by the enemy from Fort Union, and after three battles with them, all of us who were not killed or taken prisoners were obliged to destroy everything they had, and flee to the mountains for their lives, and get out of the country, the Lord only knows how. We were among those who were taken prisoners. John White, your cousin, was killed at the battle of Fort Craig. He fell by my side, and then I first thought of what you had told me, but it was too late. I had a finger shot off, but went on up the country with the rest.

Our company, with the Second and Third regiments, reached Santa Fe the 16th or 17th of March. In two days our regiment came up. We were to wait a short time, and then march on and take Fort Union, which we thought ours already, and then New Mexico would belong to the new government of the South, and it then would be so easy to cut off all communication from California. On the 22d, six hundred of us were ordered to march to Apache canon to stand picket. Here we were all dismounted and our horses sent to a ranche, on account of their being worn out by hard riding. One company went with the horses to guard them, and we went into camp on a ranch at the mouth of the canon. On the twenty-sixth, we got word that the enemy were coming down the canon, in the shape of two hundred Mexicans and about two hundred regulars. Out we marched with two cannon, expecting an easy victory, but what a mistake. Instead of Mexicans and regulars, they were regular demons, that iron and lead had no effect upon, in the shape of Pike's Peakers from the Denver City Gold mines, where we thought of going to about a year ago. As I said, up the canon we went for four miles, when we met the enemy coming at double quick, but the grape and shell soon stopped them, but before we could form in line of battle, their infantry were upon the hills, on both sides of us, shooting us down like sheep. The order was given to retreat down the canon, which we did for about a mile. There the cannon and a company of the men on both sides. In these mountains, about one hundred and fifty men were stationed. Forty more were stationed in and about some houses on the right of the road; I among the number. The rest were drawn up in line of battle across the road. This was no sooner done than up came the cannon with the enemy a their heels, but when they saw us ready to receive them, they stopped; but only for a short time, for in a few moments they could be seen on the mountains, jumping from rock to rock like so many sheep. They had no sooner got within shooting distance of us, than up came a company of cavalry at full charge, with swords and revolvers drawn, looking like so many flying devils. On they came to what I supposed certain destruction, but nothing like lead or iron seemed to stop them, for we were pouring it into them from every side like hail in a storm. In a moment these devils had run the gauntlet for a half mile, and were fighting hand to hand with our men in the road. The houses that I spoke of before, were seven or eight hundred yards to the right of the road, with a wide ditch between it and them. Here we felt safe, but again we were mistaken, for no sooner did they see us, than some of them turned their horses, jumped the ditch, and like demons, came charging on us. It looked as if their horses' feet never touched the ground, until they were among us.

It was a grand sight. We were shooting as fast as we could, and to see that handful of men jump the ditch and charging on us; we expected to shoot the last one, before they reached us. But luck was against us, and after fighting hand to hand with them, and our comrades being shot and cut down every moment, we were obliged to surrender.

Now who do you suppose it was that came charging and nearly running over me, with a revolver pointed at my head, and ordered me to lay down my arms and consider myself a prisoner—which I did—for I knew the next moment would be my last if I did not? It was George Lowe, brother-in-law of Mr. Whitney, that keeps store in Portage, Wisconsin. You know him well, I knew him as soon as I saw him, but he did not recognize me and I was very glad of it. I tried to get a chance to see him after we got to Union, but never could. I expect to see him at Fort Craig. I think he will be some surprised to see who it was that he came so near shooting. George Turner was also among the Pike's Peakers. He left Wisconsin last summer. I saw him after the fight, and he told me that he had received a letter from your folks last February, and that they were all well, and your brother had joined the Wisconsin Volunteers and gone to the war. How one of these men that charged us ever escaped death will ever be a wonder to me. Our men who were fighting with them in the road, were soon obliged to retreat, and the fight was over.

About eighty of us that were taken prisoners were soon marched off towards Fort Union. How many were killed and wounded, I don't know, but there must have been a large number. Such a sight I never want to see again. As I was marched off the field, I saw some men lying with their heads shot nearly off, and some with their arms or legs shot off, and one poor man that belonged to our company, I saw lying against a tree, with his brains all shot out. Henry Asher had an arm shot off, but made out to escape. He was standing by my side when he was shot. The men that charged us seemed to have a charmed life, for if they had not they could never have reached us alive. In a few days our number was increased by more of our men, who told us that they were reinforced the night after the first battle by 1,300 men, under Col. Scurry, from Santa Fe. The Pike's Peakers were also reinforced, and on the 28th they fought another battle near the same place as the first. After fighting all day both armies retreated. Our army marched back to Santa Fe for provisions, as our whole train of seventy wagons was burned by the enemy. In one of the wagons was that trunk of clothing you sent me while I was at Fort Filmore, It was burned up with the rest. Since then I have been furnished some clothing by our enemies, who I must say, are very good in that way. They also furnished us with very good provisions, but it goes very hard with the boys to walk as we were all mounted when we came to this country. How many were killed and wounded in both fights I cannot say, but I have been told by some of the men who were in both battles, and were taken prisoners at Santa Fe, that there were between four and five hundred killed and wounded. Our men were soon driven out of Santa Fe and Albuquerque, and made a stand at Peralta. Here they had another battle, but were again obliged to retreat, as the Pike's Peakers had made a junction with a large number of the enemy from Fort Craig. In a few days after this, they were obliged to burn the rest of their train and flee to the mountains. I hope they have reached Texas in safety. One of the men that was taken prisoner a few days after they left Peralts, tells me that out of the 3,800 men and 327 wagons that were with us when we left Fort Fillmore, only, 1,200 men and thirteen wagons remained together when they were obliged to flee to the mountians. The rest of the men must have been killed, wounded or taken prisoner. Some of the prisoners were sent to the States; the rest of us have been started home this way, by swearing never to take up arms against the United States again, which I was very glad to do, and I hope the day is not far distant when Gen. Sibley will be hung. If brother John has not joined the volunteers yet, keep him away for God's sake. Give my love to all the folks and kiss the baby for me. Had it not been for the devils from Pike's Peak, this country would have been ours. If I can get work here I will write to you again as soon as I can.

From Your Affectionate Husband,

GEORGE M. BROWN.

* * *

Excerpted from the *Denver News*, April 30, 1862, as cited in *"History of the First Regiment of Colorado Volunteers."* by Ovando J. Hollister, 1863, Thos. Gibson & Co., Publishers, Denver, C.T.

FOREWORD

If we understand correctly, the State Historical and Natural History Society of Colorado first published *The Colorado Volunteers in The Civil War* in 1906 as a paperback. We bought a copy during a visit a long time ago, and since our home and business now occupies 16 acres of the Battlefield, we of course decided to bring back the book as one of our "... Beautiful Rio Grande Classics." We published it in a facsimile library edition in 1971.

Unfortunately, the original title sort of indicated that the work was an item of Colorado history, which it is, in a way. But it also includes portions of the history of New Mexico and of Texas. Some scholars have said that had the Confederates won the Battle of Glorieta Pass, the entire course of American history might have been changed in those three remarkable days in March of 1862. For the troopers on both sides who fought in and over the New Mexico mountains, canyons and forests, it was a critical fight to determine whether Western America with its California, Colorado and Nevada goldfields stayed in the Union or joined the Confederacy. In 1906, author Jerome C. Smiley covered the possibilities that victory might have accrued to the Confederacy in his Preface that begins on page 10.

Our hardcover edition went out of print in 1975. The title with the word "Colorado" doomed the book for many New Mexicans and almost all Texans. Since then, though, times have changed a bit for the better, we believe. The three-day conflict that occurred partly in our backyard (so to speak) and roundabout for several miles east and west, has come to be regarded by many historians as a milestone in the War Between the States.

Besides these words here, we have the pleasure of including a summary of the events described in the book by New Mexico's 'Historian in Residence' and our friend, Marc Simmons who lives in Cerrillos, New Mexico. We also talked Neil Mangum out of some copy that offers a complementary perspective; what it is is *his viewpoint* in his own words. Neil is the regional historian of the National Park Service Southwest Region in the Santa Fe Regional Office. What Neil has to say relates to the maps and statistical data that so nicely illustrate the hours and minutes of the Glorieta conflict. It all occurred right here on March 26th, 27th, and 28th, one hundred and nineteen years ago this year.

We especially urge the reader to give some thoughtful time and study to the fine maps and battle statistics which so clearly illustrate what happened at Glorieta Pass those cold March days so long ago. For 35 years, a student of that portion of the history of the Civil War that occurred here, Burt Schmitz of Cupertino, Calif., has used the text of this book and of many other works that refer to this subject to reconstruct the battle in its human and military terms. He has been painstaking and careful with this extraordinary research. The appendix, the result of his efforts, reflects the men in combat as people, rather than statistics. Mr. Schmitz has simply brought into a better focus those tragic 72 hours when American soldiers fought each other, many to their death. What he has pictured with these maps and charts and data is how *he* reads and interprets the events of those sad but historic days. This small but important military engagement in the mountains of New Mexico is and properly belongs to *American* history.

To that, what can anyone say but "amen?" We extend our sincere appreciation and thanks to Burt Schmitz, to Marc Simmons and to Neil Mangum. We believe the work done for this edition will be greatly appreciated by those who find a map of help in understanding a situation that occurred many years ago, but was of considerable and much-overlooked importance in 1862 . . . and since. We ourselves consider that the work of these three scholars should greatly help the reader who likes the intimate detail of such historic events.

Robert B. McCoy

Glorieta, New Mexico
June 1991

PREFACE

More than a century and a quarter after Appomattox, we continue to pay tribute to the men, North and South, who fought in the Civil War. As an object lesson, that terrible, bloody conflict deserves our attention. It lingers in our collective memory as perhaps the most soul shattering episode in our national history. And, this "first of all modern wars," as it is often termed, persists in fascinating us.

One of the more unusual chapters in the story of the Civil War was the New Mexico Campaign of 1862. It focussed upon an invasion by Texan Confederates, who early in the year advanced northward from El Paso, fought and won the Battle of Valverde, and then subsequently seized Albuquerque and Santa Fe. A main objective of the rebels was to complete the occupation of New Mexico and use it as a springboard for launching an expedition of conquest against the flourishing goldfields of Colorado. That plan, however, was effectively derailed on March 28 at the Battle of Glorieta, fought in a wooded mountain pass fifteen miles east of Santa Fe.

In acknowledgement of its importance, as one of the turning points of the war, Glorieta has sometimes been granted the title "Gettysburg of the West." But that in no way diminishes the significance of Glorieta.

In this battle the rebels claimed victory, and so they might, since at day's end they held the battlefield and Union forces were preparing to take flight for Fort Union on New Mexico's eastern plains. Nevertheless, while the engagement had been in progress, a Federal detachment had circled five miles to the rear and burned the lightly defended Confederate supply train at Johnson's Ranch. Loss of their provisions and wagons contributed to the Texans deciding two weeks later to withdraw down the Rio Grande, abandoning the campaign.

The first effort to write a general history of these stirring events was undertaken by educator and author William C. Whitford, long a resident of Wisconsin. From an AT&SF railway car, apparently sometime in the late 1880s, he first saw the Glorieta Battlefield and had his interest aroused by a fellow passenger, an ex-soldier who had taken part in the affray. Later, Whitford made several first hand surveys of the field of action, accompanied by surviving battle participants who identified for him the locations of lines, troop movements and major events. He also made a series of photographs, which showed the battlefield before serious alterations of the terrain had occurred.

When Whitford died in 1902, his manuscript on the Colorado volunteers (who had marched south to aid in defending New Mexico) and on the Glorieta battle was nearly complete. In that condition, his heirs turned it over to the body that is today the Colorado Historical Society, which made some minor additions and published it in 1906. Ever since, Whitford's book has been regarded as a classic account of the New Mexico campaign.

This reprint by The Rio Grande Press is enhanced by the addition of supplementary material, an index (lacking in the original), and a series of highly useful field maps prepared by a long-time student of the Glorieta battle, Burt Schmitz. For all those interested in the Civil War in the far Southwest, William C. Whitford's book will continue to serve as a key reference.

Marc Simmons

Cerrillos, New Mexico
June 1991

Colorado Volunteers in the Civil War

The New Mexico Campaign in 1862

BY

WILLIAM CLARKE WHITFORD, D.D.
PRESIDENT OF MILTON COLLEGE

ILLUSTRATED

DENVER
THE STATE HISTORICAL AND NATURAL HISTORY SOCIETY
1906

PUBLICATIONS OF
THE STATE HISTORICAL AND NATURAL HISTORY SOCIETY
OF COLORADO

Historical Series. I

CONTENTS.

ILLUSTRATIONS.

PREFACE.

BY JEROME C. SMILEY.

Our Civil War was the most tremendous struggle for preservation of the national unity of a homogeneous people of which the annals of our race contain any record. Its battle-front was more than two thousand miles long, reaching from the Virginia Coast far into the large Territory of New Mexico, which, until the organization of Arizona Territory in 1863, extended westward to California. Near the western end of this unparalleled fighting-line one of the highly momentous campaigns in that great national tragedy was closed in victory for the Union early in the second year of the war.

The men in whom were the military ability and the very bone and sinew of the Union cause in that campaign, and who bore the burden of hardship and sacrifice in winning the victory which abruptly checked and turned the rising tide of Confederate successes in the Southwest, were citizen-soldiers of the Territory of Colorado.

On the part of the Confederates that campaign meant far more than appears when it is considered merely as a military enterprise— as an ambitious inroad into a section of the national domain outside the boundaries of the Southern Confederacy. Back of it was a political project of vast magnitude, upon which enthusiastic Southern leaders had set their hearts.

In 1860, 1861 and well into 1862 the militant spirit of disunion was not confined to the slave-holding States of our country. Disruption of the old Union was boldly advocated among and favored by a large and influential element of the population of California— an element that predominated in number and influence in the southern half of that State. Far-northwest Oregon had many earnest and active supporters of secession, who thought their interests demanded an independent government on the Pacific Slope. In the Territory of Utah, which then included the area of the present State of Nevada, these of its people of the Mormon persuasion had been embittered against the United States Government by reason of their long-continued embroilments with it, and were ready for any change in which immunity from interference in their church-and-domestic affairs was conceded to them. The inhabitants of New Mexico were divided in sentiment, but while probably more than one-half of them at heart were for the Union, those of the western part of the Territory (the present Arizona) were almost unanimously against it; and these, as well as the other sympathizers with the breaking-up policy, were led by men of high standing among them and of extreme determination. When the Territory of Colorado was organized in 1861, a large majority of its population was in the town of Denver, and in the Clear Creek, the Boulder and the South Park mining districts. Perhaps rather more than two-thirds of the people were loyal to the Union, but among their friends and associates and neighbors were many who were ardent and outspoken for the Southern cause. The first discovery of gold here that was followed by practical results had been made by Georgians in 1858, and a host of Southern men had come into the country in 1859 and '60. The first permanent town within the area of the Territory—one of the municipal constituents of the present City of Denver—had been founded in the autumn of 1858 largely under the leadership of Southerners. These Colorado pioneers from the South were, as a rule, men of sterling character and of much personal popularity.

In this backward glance at the political conditions existing in that period in Colorado, New Mexico, Utah, and on the Pacific Coast, we may see the reasons for the exuberant hopes that were sanguinely cherished by some Southern leaders in 1861-'62. Because of these conditions they confidently expected to split off from the Union, in addition to the States which had already seceded and formed the "Confederate States of America", these three Territories and the larger part, if not all, of the Pacific Coast proper. Their anticipations and plans embraced even more than this, for it was their intention to acquire, also, either with money or by force of arms, a large part of northern Mexico, which was to be annexed to the Southern Confederacy. Major Trevanion T. Teel, one of General Sibley's very efficient officers, in a brief account of the objects of the Confederate campaign in New Mexico in 1862 and of the

causes of its failure, written and published about twenty years ago,
said that if it had been successful,

"negotiations to secure Chihuahua, Sonora and Lower California,
either by purchase or by conquest, would be opened; the state of
affairs in Mexico made it an easy thing to take those States, and the
Mexican President would be glad to get rid of them and at the same
time improve his exchequer. In addition to all this, General Sibley intimated that there was a secret understanding between the
Mexican and the Confederate authorities, and that, as soon as our
occupation of the said States was assured, a transfer of those States
would be made to the Confederacy. Juarez, the President of the
Republic (so called), was then in the City of Mexico with a small
army under his command, hardly sufficient to keep him in his position. That date (1862) was the darkest hour in the annals of our
sister republic, but it was the brightest of the Confederacy, and
General Sibley thought that he would have little difficulty in con-
summating the ends so devoutly wished by the Confederate Government".

But we have not yet reached the limit of Southern purposes in
that memorable campaign. Confederate control of the gold-produc-
ing regions of the West then known—Colorado and California—
was another great result expected from its successful issue, and
which figured largely in the calculations. President Lincoln held
these sources of gold supply as being of vital importance to the
Union cause, as forming "the life-blood of our financial credit".
Jefferson Davis, President of the Southern Confederacy, also com-
prehended their value in that time of stress, and hoped to make them
an acceptable basis of foreign loans to his government.

It is usually unprofitable to speculate about what "might have
happened"; yet there can be no reasonable doubt that if the Confederate army which entered New Mexico at the beginning of 1862
had not been stopped and defeated at La Gloriéta, or somewhere else
in that vicinity about the same time, our histories of the War for
the Union would read differently. In their dreams of the near
future some Southern leaders saw their Confederacy extended to
the Pacific Coast and embracing more than one-half of the territory
of the United States, while in those of others it formed a junction
and an alliance with another division of the old Union—with a
"Western Confederacy" having dominion over all that part of our

country lying west of the Continental Divide, save in the south an outlet to the Pacific for the Southern people. Had General Sibley succeeded in taking Fort Union, with its large stores of arms, artillery and general military supplies, his further progress before he could have been confronted by an adequate force perhaps would have been over an easy road toward fulfillment of the plans of his government. We are further informed by Major Teel that "Sibley was to utilize the results of Baylor's successes" (see the second chapter of this volume), and that,

"with the enlistment of men from New Mexico, California, Arizona and Colorado, form an army which would effect the ultimate aim of the campaign, for there were scattered all over the Western States and Territories Southern men who were anxiously awaiting an opportunity to join the Confederate army; * * * an army of advance would be organized, and 'On to San Francisco' would be the watchword; * * *"

With the Pacific Coast in their possession by conquest, or with a free way to it by alliance with a "Western Confederacy", the world would have been open to the Confederates, since it would have been impossible for the Federal navy effectively to blockade that coast. Furthermore, the oceans could have been made to swarm with Confederate cruisers and privateers preying upon the commerce of the Union. An approach to success in this great scheme, with a prospect of the domain of the United States becoming broken into three minor nationalities, probably would have secured recognition of the Southern Confederacy from the English and French governments at once, and perhaps from others in Europe. What, then, might the consequences have been?

It was such considerations as those outlined in the foregoing that induced Confederate leaders in 1861-'62 to attempt to establish provisionally a military government in western New Mexico, and to send General Sibley forth to carry the war into the Rocky Mountains. Regarded solely from a military standpoint, the mere conquest and occupation of New Mexico, and even of Colorado in addition, could have worked no advantage of importance to the Southern Confederacy; but possession of both would have strongly fortified subsequent efforts to consummate the greater purposes. Bearing in mind these comprehensive designs, we shall be better prepared to appreciate the services rendered the Nation by the Colorado Volunteers in the New Mexico campaign in 1862.

In this volume we have the first circumstantially complete history of that campaign yet published, and no doubt the story will be a surprising revelation to many of its readers. As a military achievement the defeat of General Sibley was overshadowed by the greater conflicts of the war, and the bold political project which it caused to vanish into thin air belongs to a part of the history of that period of which but little has yet become commonly known. In a lesser war the hurried march of the Colorado Volunteers to the rescue and their desperate fighting in La Gloriéta Pass, with the great issues at stake forming the background of the scene, would have been celebrated long and far in song and story. The author, in the spirit which prompts the Union Veteran to hold out a hand and take off his hat to the Confederate Soldier, but without a thought of sympathy for the "Lost Cause", unreservedly recognizes the resolution, courage and devotion of the men who constituted Sibley's army, as well as the bravery and ability of the officers who led them. The victor could add nothing to his credit by disparaging the vanquished, even were he so disposed to do.

The first engagement in La Gloriéta Pass usually has been known in Colorado as the "Apache Cañon Fight", and the second as the "Battle of Pigeon's Ranch". The author very properly has treated the two as parts of one encounter, for which he adopted the name, "Battle of La Gloriéta". The second conflict is so called in some of the official records of the Union armies, and is known only by that name in the surviving Confederate records. While names of ranches and also of cañons are liable to change with changes of ownership of the land, "La Gloriéta", by which the locality, and the pass as a whole, have been known by the Spanish-Mexican people of New Mexico for more than two hundred years, is likely to remain attached to both indefinitely into the future. Therefore, it is eminently fitting that the bloody struggles in the pass—the Gettysburg of the Southwest—should be known by the historic name which that opening through the southern terminal heights of the Sangré dé Cristo ("Blood of Christ") Range so long has borne.

The confidence expressed by the author at the close of his valuable contribution to the written history of the West, that the time would surely come when some worthy memorial would be raised by the State of Colorado to the Civil War Volunteers of the Territory, is about to be justified. The Fifteenth General Assembly, in its regular session in 1905, provided for the erection in front of the capitol of an appropriate monument to them, and at the time of this writing its foundations have been laid.

Dr. Whitford, born in Otsego County, New York, in 1828, was educated for the ministry and ordained in 1856. In 1858 he became the Principal of Milton Academy, a promising young institution of learning at Milton, Wisconsin. Nine years later, through his ability and zeal as an educator, the academy was raised to the dignity of Milton College, and so incorporated by an act of the Wisconsin Legislature. He was elected its first President, and filled the position continuously until his death in May, 1902. He served as a member of the Wisconsin Legislature of 1868; was State Superintendent of Public Instruction for two consecutive terms (1878-'81), and for a number of years was a member of the Board of Regents of the State University of Wisconsin. He was the author of various studies of the early history of Wisconsin, and made many explorations of prehistoric mounds and other earthworks in that State.

Dr. Whitford's death occurred before he had had opportunity to obtain from Colorado records some further facts he required for this volume, and when his manuscript was received by our Historical Society it was seen that he had carefully noted the several deficiencies. The more important of the lacking data were the names of the killed and of the wounded among the Colorado Volunteers in the New Mexico campaign, and those of their company officers; the remainder having relation to sundry details and to some requested verifications. His notations respecting these matters received faithful attention from the Society. About one-half of the illustrations are from photographs procured by the author in New Mexico, most of which he caused to be made while he was on the ground; the rest, with a few exceptions, were drawn from the Society's resources.

Denver, June, 1906.

William Clarke Whitford, D. D.
(From a photograph in the State Historical and Natural History Society's collection.)

INTRODUCTORY.

In a springtime some years ago I made my first visit into the unique and romantic region of New Mexico, for the purpose of viewing its varied and impressive scenery, and especially of seeing its many places of historical interest. The railway ride on the last day, through the southeastern quarter of Colorado and on to Santa Fé, in the crystalline atmosphere and the brilliant sunshine, was fascinating in a very remarkable degree. The forenoon hours were occupied by the train in crossing an almost treeless expanse of rolling plains and low mésas, in full sight of the Spanish peaks to the west—those outlying sentinels of the famous Sangré dé Cristo range. In the afternoon it dragged its way southward along the border of the immense plains, which sweep in on the left and then across the roadway to the base of gray foothills, which at some points are close at hand and at others many miles distant; and its course afforded a complete view on the right of an almost continuous series of lofty and snow-covered pinnacles, which gave a ragged edge to the horizon. The train crept between the inferior eminences, composed of Post-tertiary strata of compact sandstone, named Fisher's peak and Simpson's rest, and capped with huge cube-like masses of dark grayish rock, the remains of a stupendous volcanic overflow that preceded the upheaval of these towering ridges. It then plunged into a winding cañon, following the course of a rushing creek. As it climbed the heavy grade in the Raton pass, across which runs the boundary line between Colorado and New Mexico, we had hurried, but inspiring, glances into deep gorges on one side, views of the swelling of almost barren heights over and beyond each other on the opposite side into the dark blue sky, and a magnificent backward look, through the narrow cañon, to the twin Spanish peaks in the distance, clothed on their slopes with rich purple color, and wearing on their heads, as touched by the sunlight, crowns of brilliant silvery whiteness.

2   (17)

Then the train entered a tunnel at the summit of this mountain range, which projects miles into the plains, and, on emerging from it, descended swiftly to the ordinary level of the high table-land, on which, for a long stretch, were feeding flocks of sheep and herds of cattle, and stopped at least a score of times at small hamlets and old settled towns, which showed a strange mixture of wretched adobe huts and modern wooden structures, and also of various types of Mexican and American inhabitants. The eye rested frequently upon the well-worn old Santa Fé trail, which runs here, as back in the Arkansas valley, parallel to the railroad, and on which were slowly drawn along, each by two or three double teams, a few lumbering, canvas-top freight wagons, loaded with supplies for some mining camps or for live-stock ranches. They were the relics of the caravans of pack horses and "prairie schooners" that had traveled hitherward from the Missouri river almost from the beginning of the nineteenth century. Skirting around the lower terminus of the imperial Rockies, whose bold heads, lifted into the clouds, line northward almost three thousand miles, the train approached, just before the darkening shadows of evening were falling upon the weird but splendid landscape, a narrow, transverse opening between the mountains, which forms at the west a side valley of the upper Pécos river. This is known as La Gloriéta pass; though often designated as the Apache cañon, from a powerful tribe of roving Indians who terrorized this region and the country to the southwest for centuries.

Just at this point, as the engine was laboriously drawing the train in a northwesterly direction toward the summit of this thoroughfare, a gentleman on board, inviting a group of passengers to stand around him on the front platform of a coach, said to them with much earnestness: "Right in here were some battles of the Civil War." "Between whom?" one of the party inquired. "Confederate and Union soldiers," was his answer. "Whereabouts in here?" another asked. "At several places in this pass," he responded; "but the severest one was down among those trees along the arroyo, and on these slopes you see, and near that large adobe building yonder." "This is surprising; we never heard of these engagements before," several remarked. "Very likely," he continued: "for I think that not one person in ten thousand in the states east of us knows to-day anything about them or of the campaign in which they were fought." "Is there any account of them in our school histories or in the popular magazines?" he was questioned. "Probably not," he replied; "but you can accept my statement as true, for I fired at the invaders myself for hours with my Colorado company, in the woods down here, and from behind those

A Landscape in the Glorieta Locality.
(From one of the author's photographs.)

rocks on the ridge over there. I was never in so hot a contest before or afterward in the Civil War." The conversation was interrupted by the train reaching the station at the small hamlet of Gloriéta, and by our Colorado train-acquaintance leaving us there. Later we learned that during this conflict the camp of the Northern army was about six miles back in the Pécos valley, and that that of the Southern was at the western end of the pass. In the deep depression from one place to the other the maneuvers of both armies, as well as their encounters, in this mountain region, were confined almost entirely.

A superficial examination of the history of the events just mentioned brought to light, in main part, the causes of the ignorance above alleged. At the time they occurred, early in the spring of 1862, they failed to attract the notice of the American people. The means of communication from the Southwest to news centers in the East were slow and imperfect, the nearest telegraph line—one of a single wire—being at Denver City. This expedition of these loyal troops was largely independent of other operations of the Union armies. Public attention then was intensely fixed upon the gigantic preparations of the forces under General McClellan for the Peninsular campaign in Virginia. Three weeks before, the Monitor had disabled the Merrimac in Hampton Roads. Fort Donelson had already been taken, and the fierce struggle at Shiloh happened a week and a half later. New Orleans surrendered to Farragut less than a month afterward. Furthermore, the number of soldiers on both sides engaged here was insignificant in comparison with the tens and hundreds of thousands who were then fighting on eastern battlefields. But their heroism, their powers of endurance and the unprecedented scope of their achievements have challenged the highest admiration of all acquainted with their deeds. The Confederate troops marched a distance approaching one thousand miles over a wide stretch of arid country in Texas, beside over three hundred and fifty miles outside of their state, up the Rio Grandé valley, with its scant population, to reach this pass; and Federal troops, over three hundred miles, along the eastern base of the Rocky mountains, still in the grasp of winter, with its terrific storms. Yet the immediate and permanent results of the victory gained here were among the most conspicuous and valuable to the Union that were won during the war. Here was utterly defeated, in a very brief time, the bold and comprehensive scheme of the Southern Confederacy to acquire, by invasion and force of arms, the possession and control of all this southwestern mountainous country, including its forts, passes and towns, and to extend this possession northward to Denver, Colorado, and thence westward to Salt Lake City, Utah. But another purpose in this great scheme was to open, through New Mexico (which then embraced the present Arizona, also), access to

California—to secure "a pathway to the Pacific Coast," the harbors of which could not then be easily blockaded by the Federal navy. They desired thus to attach to their domain all this vast region, and to secure thereby the adherence and support of its Indian tribes, Mexicans, and of thousands of active sympathizers who had either emigrated from the South or were reared elsewhere and approved of the extension of negro slavery. In case of their final separation from the Northern states, their government, the Confederacy, would bar the latter from any further growth westward, and ultimately assume the charge of the Asiatic commerce of this continent. However impracticable or idealistic such a project may now appear, there is ample evidence that it was then seriously entertained and its realization confidently expected by them. In fact, it was the cause of their loss of immense treasure and the death of many heroic, but misguided, soldiers of their army. Had their failure been postponed for some months, and had they gained supremacy also over a score of other natural fortresses in the mountains, and enlisted, as they wished, their allies in defense of these, it would have required a vast Union army to dislodge them, and years of struggle to regain the allegiance of the inhabitants.

The disastrous result of this episode of the Civil War to the South adds another most interesting chapter to the history of the upper Pécos valley and of La Gloriéta pass. The route through both these, and the less important one through the former and into the San Cristobal cañon, immediately to the southwest, have been to the development of New Mexico and adjacent territory what the celebrated Brenner pass in the Alps has been to that of central-southern Europe since ancient times. For hundred of years before and since this continent became known to the civilized world here was the chief passageway of the nomads and village aborigines of this region through these immense mountain ranges, and here has been the scene of repeated and murderous attacks among them. The earliest Spanish explorers, beginning back in the first half of the sixteenth century, traveled through here on their visits to friendly tribes and on their journeys into the great western plains. Mexican families in the valley of the Rio Grandé found here a convenient exit for themselves to the opposite side of these lofty and crowded peaks, when they settled there to the northward in such towns as Las Végas, Raton, Trinidad and La Junta. The Santa Fé trail ran through here, and previous to the time in which the

Southern Side of the Ruined Pecos Mission.
(From one of the author's photographs.)

railroad took its place long trains of heavy wagons could be seen traversing its steep inclines. In 1841, and two years afterward, hostile or plundering expeditions from Texas, then an independent republic, became associated with this pass in their prospective raids on the town of Santa Fé. General Manuel Armijo, who had been governor of New Mexico for several terms, stationed in its extreme western part his native troops of about 4,000, occupying an advantageous position, which he fortified by some earthworks and fallen trees, for the purpose of intercepting and "annihilating" General Stephen W. Kearny and his United States forces, on their way in 1846 to take possession of the province, then a part of the territory of the Republic of Mexico. Armijo's project was ingloriously abandoned, and the invading army marched through unmolested and on to Santa Fé, which capitulated without any bloodshed. Subsequently, in the same year, Colonel Sterling Price, with his famous Missouri regiment, followed the same route when he suppressed an insurrection of some of the inhabitants of the province. Colonel A.

W. Doniphan, in 1847, led his command through these gorges on his expedition to capture Chihuahua, in northern Mexico.

The name, "Gloriéta," was bestowed upon this locality by the Spanish settlers of New Mexico at an early day. It was suggested by dense and beautiful growths of cottonwood and pine trees then on the land that long afterward became Pigeon's ranch, and also along the arroyo and up the slopes. Later it was given to the round-top eminence—Gloriéta mountain—seen to the west soon after one enters the pass from the opposite direction; then to the pass itself, and to the cañon at its eastern opening, and to the local station (elevation, 7,587 feet) of the Santa Fé Railway when that road was built. Since then it has been assigned to this entire section in praise of its picturesque scenery, genial climate and interesting traditions. The pass at each extremity is very narrow, but in the middle nearly a quarter of a mile wide. On both flanks it is shut in by irregular crests, which rise above its bottom generally from one to two thousand feet. Its abrupt sides are thinly covered with cedar bushes and stunted oaks and pines. In its eastern half, particularly along the arroyo, are now growing only a few large cottonwoods, and close to them some yellow pines—the remnants of the Gloriéta forest, which adorned the locality as late as forty years ago.

When copious rains occur in this region two streams have their origin in the watershed at the summit, near the middle of the pass, one taking a southeasterly course by Pigeon's ranch, and emptying at last into the Pécos river, and the other a southwesterly course, becoming a head of the Galistéo, a small branch of the Rio Grandé. About three miles below Cañoncito, at the farthest end of the pass, the second stream has worn a deep, very narrow and tortuous channel through the solid rock, which the Santa Fé Railway Company has designated also Apache cañon. The trains run through this defile at the end of a long and rapid descent.

About nine miles to the east, in a parklike and undulating valley, close to the old Santa Fé trail, and in sight of this railroad, a mile and a half to the south, are the gray ruins of a famous ancient village of Pueblo Indians, called the Pécos Pueblo, and near them the reddish ones of a Catholic mission, commonly known as the "Pécos Church." They are situated not far from the center of an apparent amphitheatre, seven miles in width and twelve in length, and surrounded, on the one hand, by tree-covered mésas, whose level tops are two thousand feet above their base, and on the other by mountains, which rise four thousand feet above their lowest foothills and present timbered slopes and craggy summits. A visit to the site of this ruined old pueblo would reveal more clearly to the reader that it lies in one of the most romantic and delightful retreats, in a region where the plains and the snowy elevations, crowded together, vie with each other for the mastery. The former have pushed themselves, like an entering wedge, some distance in among the latter.

View of Part of the Ruins of the Great Pecos Pueblo.
(From one of the author's photographs.)

Here are seen the demolished walls of perhaps the largest aboriginal stone dwelling ever erected within the United States, and not inferior in size and capacity for sheltering human beings to the greatest of the old Aztec structures in Mexico and Central America. The visitor still may enter the dilapidated mission edifices, which are said to have been the most capacious and substantial ever dedicated by the early Franciscan friars to the introduction of Christianity among the Pueblo tribes in the Southwest. These buildings were located on the highest portion of a ridge of ground running over a third of a mile from the south to the north, shaped like an irregular and elongated flint spearhead, spread over at most places with a thin layer of sandy and micaceous soil, underlaid by compact, brownish-gray limerock of the new red sandstone formation, and rising almost a hundred feet above the beds of two streams, often dry, one a few rods distant to the west and the other to the east.

The camp of the Union soldiers who won the victory of La Gloriéta was near the site of these destroyed buildings of a bygone era.

When I first visited the locality I was deeply impressed by what I saw and heard. Now, having well in mind the stirring, but little-known, events of the Civil War which are identified with it, I resolved to return and go more carefully over the places where the fighting occurred, and to prepare for publication, as faithfully as I could do so, an account of that campaign. Upon subsequent visits I was accompanied in my excursions by some men who were eye-witnesses of the principal military operations here, and by others who had been for many years very familiar with active participants in them.

PRELIMINARY CONFEDERATE PLANS AND OPERA-TIONS IN THE SOUTHWEST.

For a year or so before South Carolina seceded, Mr. John B. Floyd, secretary of war in President Buchanan's cabinet, caused to be sent to various army posts in the South and the Southwest vast quantities of military supplies in great variety, and of this prepara-tory distribution of the materials of war New Mexico received a large share, designed chiefly for the use of soldiers of the South when the contemplated Confederacy should attempt to establish its authority over the Southwest and into the country that soon after-ward became the territory of Colorado. He also caused to be moved into New Mexico an unusually large number of soldiers of the regular army, under the command, to a great extent, of officers from the Southern states. It was expected that these officers would influence the people of that territory to favor and aid materially the secession movement, and that when the proper time had arrived they would resign their positions and accept commissions in the Southern army. It was also the intention that they should persuade the soldiers of their commands to abandon their flag and enlist under that of the new government.

At the time the Southern states began to secede, the people of that part of New Mexico now the territory of Arizona were known to be almost unanimous in their support of the movement. In a con-vention held at Tucson in 1861 they formally annexed their part of the country to the Confederacy, and elected a delegate to its con-gress. The mass of the people of the territory, a large majority of whom lived in the Rio Grandé valley, evidently were rather apa-thetic in their attachment to the Union, and some of their former territorial officers were bitterly antagonistic. California had a strong element which sustained the Southern cause. Colorado had, as reported, as many as 7,500 inhabitants—about one-third of the population—who were openly or secretly disloyal to the national government. The assertion was made that "the Mormons in Utah,

Colonel Edward R. S. Canby, Commander of the Union Forces in New Mexico in 1861-62.

(From a wood engraving, from an after-the-war photograph, in "Battles and Leaders of the Civil War." The Century Company, 1887.)

if a chance were given them, would heartily join the enemies of the Northern states." Several powerful and warlike tribes of Indians in the West, and others in the Southwest, could be incited to fiercer hostility against the troops employed to keep them in subjection. A series of bold achievements on battlefields and in marches in these territories by Southern troops, with the expulsion of the Federal dragoons and infantry from these rugged mountains and wide-spreading plains, undoubtedly would unite and strengthen this mixed and scattered population in contesting any further settlement and jurisdiction of the North within their bounds.

The ordinance of secession adopted by Texas on February 1, 1861, went into effect on March 2d, and the state began at once to recruit and organize troops to occupy the Federal forts within its own limits, and also those in New Mexico. Those in the former were totally abandoned in the spring and summer of that year by the United States forces.

On the 22d of March Colonel William W. Loring, a native of North Carolina, an Indian fighter in Florida and Oregon, and a veteran of the Mexican War, was assigned the command of the United States troops in New Mexico, with headquarters at Santa Fé. He resigned his position about three months afterward, and joined the Texan leaders, whose plans to invade the territory he had already encouraged.

In the meantime the war department at Washington had learned of this movement, and it soon instructed Colonel Edward R. S. Canby, of the Nineteenth regiment United States Infantry, who had assumed the command thus relinquished, to make vigorous preparations to resist any such movement. Colonel Canby was born in Kentucky in 1819; early removed with his parents to Indiana; graduated at West Point in 1839; served as a lieutenant in the Seminole War from 1839 to 1842; brevetted for gallantry in five battles in the Mexican War; became major in the regular infantry in 1855, and colonel in 1861. At the close of the Civil War he was brevetted brigadier-general in the regular army "for gallant and meritorious services at the battle of Valverdé, New Mexico;" and on April 11, 1873, while commanding the Division of the Pacific, was treacherously killed by the Modoc Indians when holding a conference with them near the "lava beds" in Oregon.

Early in July, 1861, several companies of artillery and mounted rifles from Texas, commanded by Lieutenant-Colonel John R. Baylor, entered New Mexico by the way of El Paso. In the course of

Lieutenant-Colonel John R. Baylor, Commander of the first Confederate troops that invaded New Mexico.
(From a war-time photograph in the State Historical and Natural History Society's collection.)

a month the military posts in the lower part of the Rio Grande valley in New Mexico, except Fort Craig, garrisoned by United State troops, were evacuated, and so fell into the hands of these invaders. By the close of September the latter had defeated small detachments of the former in four skirmishes in this valley. These were at Mésilla and Comada Alamosa, and near Forts Thorn and Craig.

along the Rio Grandé and chiefly on its west side. In the first two the contest was the more serious. Immediately after that at Mésilla Major Isaac Lynde, of the Federal army and in charge of Fort Fillmore, situated eight miles directly south of Las Cruces, after basely abandoning his post and fleeing to San Augustine Springs, twenty-five miles distant in the Organ mountains, surrendered on July 27th, probably through cowardice, without firing a shot, and against the protests of his officers, his entire command of at least 500 men, well armed, accustomed as regulars to stern warfare and "eager for the fray," to Colonel Baylor, with a detachment of less than 300 troops. This disaster opened southern New Mexico to the invaders, and compelled Colonel Canby to gather all his forces in this region at Fort Craig; and, after enlarging and strengthening it very materially, he made it the initial point of his offensive and defensive operations during the remainder of the campaign.

Lieutenant-Colonel Baylor issued, August 1st, a proclamation to the people of the lower half of the territory. In it he stated that he took possession of this entire region "in the name and behalf of the Confederate States of America;" that he designated Mésilla as its seat of government, and that in organizing it temporarily he appointed all of its civil officers. Subsequently he announced that his jurisdiction also included practically the whole upper half of the territory of New Mexico.

In modification as well as in support of this act Jefferson Davis, the president of the Southern Confederacy, issued, February 14, 1862, his proclamation, which had been authorized by the Confederate congress on the 21st of January preceding, declaring the New Mexico country to be organized as the "territory of Arizona," its civil and military officers to be appointed by him. Among those designated by President Davis was Lieutenant-Colonel Baylor, who was named as the military governor of the territory and also as the commander of the Confederate army operating in it. Thereupon, as the executive, Colonel Baylor sent forth, March 1, 1862, another proclamation, reaffirming many terms of the first, and designating the upper boundary of the Confederate "territory of Arizona" at the thirty-fourth parallel of north latitude, which gave it less than

Brigadier-General Henry H. Sibley, Commander of the Confederate
Forces in New Mexico in 1862.

(From a wood engraving, from a war-time photograph, in "Battles
and Leaders of the Civil War." The Century Company, 1887.)

half of the entire area of New Mexico. Our story has little further to do with the Confederate "territory of Arizona" and with the energetic Colonel Baylor as its "military governor." Both continued to figure for a few months longer, and then went out with the collapse of the Confederate cause in the Southwest.

Among the officers of the United States army stationed in that section at the outbreak of the Civil War was another very able and influential man, Major Henry H. Sibley, who resigned his commission on May 13, 1861, and entered at once the service of the Confederacy. He was a Louisianian and a gradute at West Point; became a lieutenant in the operations against the Seminole Indians in Florida, and a captain of dragoons while engaged in the military occupation of Texas, and was promoted major for gallantry in the principal battles under General Winfield Scott in the Mexican War. He served in Kansas during the "free-soil" troubles, was sent twice to Utah with troops to quell Mormon disturbances, resisted the raids of the Navajo Indians in New Mexico, and superintended the construction of Fort Union, with its arsenal and storage buildings, the most complete in the territory. He wrote on June 12, 1861, from El Paso, Texas, to Colonel Loring at Santa Fé, assuring him that safe transportation could be secured from that place to New Orleans, but entreated him to delay his departure from New Mexico "a week or two," so as to prevent any of the troops still under his charge from capturing or destroying in that time "the full supplies of subsistence and ammunition" stored at El Paso for the use of Texas cavalry on their way, doubtless, from San Antonio. He regretted that he did not bring with him "the rank and file" of his entire command. But he and other disaffected officers soon learned that nearly all of the private soldiers of the Federal troops in New Mexico had resolved to remain firmly loyal to the Union.

On the 8th of July following, Sibley, as a brigadier-general, was charged at Richmond, Virginia, with the "duty of driving the Federal troops" from New Mexico, and of securing therein "all the arms, supplies and materials of war." This honor was conferred because of his recent service in the Rio Grandé valley and to the

west of it, and of his "knowledge of that country and its people."
He was instructed to proceed without delay to Texas, for the purpose of raising, as speedily as possible, a brigade to accomplish these
objects, and, if successful, also of organizing in northern New Mexico a military government.

Not until December 14th of that year was he prepared to assume
in person at Fort Bliss, a large and well-built fort, then on the Rio
Grandé at El Paso, and within the state of Texas, the command of

Fort Bliss.
(From a wood engraving in "El Gringo; or, New Mexico and Her People," by
W. W. H. Davis, 1857.)

the forces he had enlisted, and then designated as "the Army of
New Mexico," but afterward usually called "Sibley's Brigade."
These consisted, when united, of three regiments of mounted infantry, five companies under the charge of Lieutenant-Colonel Baylor, two batteries and three independent companies—a total of
nearly 3,500 men. No volunteers more hardy, courageous and
efficient ever entered the service of the Confederacy. On the 20th
of this December General Sibley addressed a proclamation to the
people of New Mexico, stating that, "by geographical position, by
similarity of institutions, by commercial interests, and by future
destinies," the territory "pertains" to the South. In it he appealed,
"in the name of former friendship," to his "old comrades in arms"

3

still in the ranks of the Union's defenders, to renounce allegiance to "the usurpers of their government and liberties," and to aid in enforcing permanently the authority he represented. He further asserted: "I am empowered to receive you into the service of the Confederate states—the officers upon their commissions, the men upon their enlistments." He declared that, by virtue of the power vested in him, he abrogated the "laws of the United States levying taxes upon the people," whose co-operation he solicited.

While this movement was in progress Colonel Canby, in whose hands were placed all of the Federal military affairs in New Mexico, made strenuous efforts during the summer and fall to counteract it within the sphere of his command. He enlarged and strengthened greatly the defensive works at Fort Craig, situated at a sharp bend in the Rio Grande; he reenforced its garrison with regular and volunteer troops, and he supplied it with the needed army stores. He sought to protect adequately the government depot at Albuquerqué. The barracks at Santa Fé received other companies of soldiers. He gave attention to guarding more securely fortified posts somewhat beyond the upper border of the territory. Fort Union was selected as the most effective center for resisting attacks in its northern portion. As was the case with most of the military posts on the western frontier, Fort Union had been located and built with a view of affording protection against attack by Indians, but not against that of a trained army of white men. Therefore, Colonel Canby ordered constructed near the old post a strong and extensive earthwork fortification, with well-protected storage facilities, into which the munitions of war and the more valuable of the other property were removed. He also provided the post with an increased force, and directed its officers to be on their guard against surprise by a Confederate force which he anticipated might enter New Mexico from Texas by way of either the Pécos or the Canadian river, to cooperate with General Sibley. Beside the great store of army supplies at the post for the use of the United States troops, valued at about $275,000 in Eastern prices, and which had been wagoned across the plains at heavy expense, Fort Union was, in the colonel's opinion, the military key to the whole situation, and therefore must be held at all hazards.

In 1861 the militia of New Mexico, practically unorganized, consisted of about 1,000 men, but the loyal people of the territory promptly undertook the enlistment and organization of several regiments—the First, Second, Third, Fourth and Fifth New Mexico Volunteers—the officers of which largely were native New Mexicans, most of them being men of ability and dauntless courage. By the close of that year the ranks of two of these regiments were nearly complete as to number of men, those of the others being only partly filled. But, to the great mortification of their officers, the majority of these troops later proved unreliable in the presence of the enemy in an engagement.

Toward the end of the year Colonel Canby requested the governor of the territory of Colorado to send him some reenforcements, and in December two companies of Colorado volunteer infantry set out upon their march to his assistance.

CONDITIONS IN COLORADO TERRITORY IN 1861.

The political conditions in Colorado at the outbreak of our Civil War were comparable, in many respects, to those existing at the same time in the states of Kentucky and Missouri. As in those states, a large number, though not a majority, of the people were in sympathy with the movement for a dissolution of the Union. The initial development of the gold diggings of the territory, some three years before, was the work of men from the South, and meanwhile the prospects for speedily acquiring modest fortunes from its mountains and gulches had attracted thither several thousands of other men from that section of our country. Among these were many who became leading spirits in the mining camps and in the primitive towns. But there, as elsewhere all over the North, during the memorable winter of 1860-61, the more conservative of the people had hoped that the nation would not be plunged into the horrors of civil war—that some means of peaceful settlement of the difficulties would yet be found. The admission of Kansas as a state, in January, 1861, with its present boundaries, left for several months the western part of the former territory of Kansas, which had extended to the Continental divide and embraced the Pike's Peak gold region, without any form of organized lawful government—a "No Man's Land."

The territory of Colorado was created by an act of congress, which became a law on February 28, 1861. Fortunately, the first governor of the new territory, Major William Gilpin, was a man of foresight and energy, and of marked intelligence, courage and patriotism. He was born on the battlefield of Brandywine, in south-eastern Pennsylvania, October 4, 1813, and had ancestors who distinguished themselves in England under Cromwell, and others who did likewise under Washington in our War of the Revolution. He was graduated by the University of Pennsylvania and also by the United States Military Academy at West Point. He saw hard serv-

William Gilpin, First Governor of Colorado Territory.
(From an after-the-war small steel engraving in the State Historical and Natural
History Society's collection.)

ice in fighting Indians in Florida and in the Far West, and joined
Colonel Doniphan's expedition into Mexico in 1847, serving as a
major in a Missouri regiment. Before and after this service with
Doniphan he made exploring tours, at least two score times, across
the Rocky mountains at various points and through the country
west to the Pacific Coast. He represented the earliest settlers in
the Willamette valley in Oregon before congress, urging its members to provide a territorial government for them, and became the
founder of the city of Portland in the mouth of this valley, near
the Columbia river. Few public men, if any, ever appreciated more
highly the importance to the United States of the vast region he so
often traversed. To the executive office he held at the outbreak of
our Civil War President Lincoln appointed him on March 22, 1861.
He served as governor of the territory of Colorado until May, 1862,
when he was removed in consequence of circumstances which are
briefly recounted on a following page. He remained a citizen of
the territory and of its successor state until his lamented death,
which occurred in the night of January 19, 1894, at his residence in
the city of Denver.

Governor Gilpin arrived in Denver City, the capital of the new
territory, on May 29, 1861, and proceeded at once to organize its
government, the first lawful one which the people of the country
may be said to have had. On assuming the duties of his position
he found among the inhabitants what he characterized as "a strong
and malignant secession element," which had been "ably and
secretly organized from November" of the previous year. Later
he wrote that "extreme and extraordinary measures" were required
"to meet and control its onslaught."

Up to the winter of 1860-61 the formal military strength of the
Pike's Peak country had not been awe-inspiring. At the beginning
of 1861 it consisted of two Denver City militia companies, which
had been organized under an "act" of the "legislature" of "Jefferson territory" authorizing a military establishment for "Governor"
Steele. One of these was the Auraria (West Denver) "Jefferson
Rangers," commanded by Captain H. H. C. Harrison, and the

other the "Denver Guards," under the command of W. P. McClure, the postmaster, and an ardent and outspoken adherent to the Southern cause. But these had disbanded early in the spring of 1861, soon after the news of the creation of the territory of Colorado by congress had been received at Denver City.

On April 24th an emblem of the new government that had arisen in the Southern states was run up over the general merchandise store of Wallingford & Murphy, on the principal business street in Denver City. Within a few minutes the vicinity was crowded by excited and angry men, who declared that the flag of disunion should not float in the town. There were others who thought it should and would, and a riot seemed near at hand. But the Union men outnumbered the others and demanded the flag's quick removal. Without standing upon ceremony, Samuel M. Logan, who soon afterward became a captain in the First regiment of Colorado Volunteers, got on top of the building, and hauled the flag down before it had fluttered long enough to smooth out its creases and wrinkles, and never again was a Confederate flag flung to the breeze in Denver City.

Captain Samuel M. Logan.
(From a war-time photograph in the State Historical and Natural History Society's collection.)

So it was that when Governor Gilpin went to Colorado to inaugurate civil government in the territory, he found its loyal people in a trying situation, one calling for prompt and decisive action by courageous and steadfast men. They were isolated by six hundred miles of rolling plains that lay between them and the borderland of the settled parts of the country to the east; menaced by Southern influences, which were conspiring and plotting to drag the territory and all the Southwest into the domain of the Confederacy; and surrounded by hordes of Indians, to whose nostrils the scent of civil war among the people whom they regarded as their worst enemies was as a sweet incense.

The United States marshal of Colorado, appointed with Gilpin, made in the summer of 1861, as required by the law creating the territory, a census of its population, exclusive of Indians, which was completed by September. According to this enumeration, which was thought to be very close, there were 18,136 white males over 21 years of age, 2,622 under 21 years, 4,484 women, and 89 negroes, a total of 25,331.

The evident need of immediate action to save Colorado to the Union, as well as the necessity of extending help to New Mexico in resisting attack from Texas, constrained Governor Gilpin to proceed soon after his arrival to the organization of troops for the defense of the two territories. Grave hindrances other than those due to Confederate sympathizers were encountered by him. Proper equipment and general supplies for soldiers were exceedingly scarce in his territory, and the "sinews of war" were almost entirely lacking. The territorial government started with a weak treasury, and among its meager contents there was next to nothing with which to provide for troops in a campaign. Absorbed in his devotion to the Union, and appreciating the gravity of the situation, he gave his government more of the character of a military than of a civil establishment, and drove ahead in doing what he thought should and must be done.

One of his early precautionary measures was to send agents forth among the people to buy guns of any sort, wherever they could be found, paying, or promising to pay, high prices for them. As most of the men in the country had either a rifle or a heavy shot gun, a comparatively large number of such arms was soon collected, but as scarcely any two were alike they were poorly adapted for use by organized troops. However, his purpose partly was to "head off" the "malignant secession element" from obtaining arms of any kind, and partly to have a supply of such weapons in case an emergency arose in which better ones were not at hand.

In this enterprise the governor soon had very active competition. The Confederate sympathizers in Denver City and its vicinity, while they had been outwardly more quiet since the flag episode of the preceding April, were by no means idle. Their leaders were resolute men, who believed firmly in the righteousness of their cause. Having been advised of the preparations for and avowed purpose of the Confederate movement into New Mexico—that of detaching the Southwest from the Union and of making Colorado a subsequent objective—they had begun organizing, or trying to as best they could without making their movements unduly conspicuous, a force to co-operate with the expected invasion from the South. They found it easier to enroll themselves than to procure materials of war. Equipping a military force in a community in which the plotters are in minority is a difficult thing to do. These men could not bring in arms and munitions from outside in any considerable number or quantity, for there were no available sources from which to draw them, and if there had been, the chances were that any such shipments would be discovered and seized by the vigilant Union men. But when Governor Gilpin began buying miscellaneous arms they threw off restraint, and entered the field for the purchase of rifles and shot guns wherever they could obtain them, together with ammunition to make the weapons effective. They went even so far as to post printed notices in the mining camps and elsewhere in the vicinity of Denver City, in which they named places where good prices would be paid for guns, powder, and so forth, mentioning an especial desire for a supply of percussion caps. It was asserted that they had also planned to raid the bank and minting establishment of Clark, Gruber & Company, as well as the larger mercantile houses, in Denver City, for the purpose of capturing gold, which they intended to contribute to the Confederate war fund. Whatever else may be thought or said of them, they certainly were a determined and fearless group of men. They succeeded in sending out a few small detachments or squads of marauders to intercept supply trains from the Missouri river, but these accomplished nothing of noteworthy importance.

Early in the autumn the Southern men who were determined at once to take up arms in behalf of the Confederate cause began to leave Colorado quietly and unostentatiously as individuals, and not as an organized military body marching forth with the pomp and circumstance of war. A large number of them thus departed and entered the Confederate armies, and served in them throughout the struggle. They had the courage of their convictions. Yet it was believed by some Union men that among those who remained longer there existed two full companies, secretly organized, that awaited the time and opportunity to act as auxiliaries to the Confederate invasion of the Southwest.

A tragic story was told in Denver City the next year of the fate of a few men who left the territory in 1861 and joined the Southern forces, and started to return some months later. This small party, of which W. P. McClure, heretofore mentioned, was a member, went to the army of General Sterling Price. They persuaded General Price that they could easily raise a Confederate regiment in Colorado. Therefore, commissions were obtained for enough of them, including McClure, to make a full complement of regimental officers; and they, with a few others, who expected to become company officers, set out across the plains for Colorado early in 1862, to recruit the regiment. The Federal authorities heard of the movement, and sent a mounted detachment of enlisted Osage Indian scouts to capture or destroy the band of newly-fledged Confederate officers. According to the story, the party was intercepted on the southeastern plains, and in the fight that ensued its every man was killed, and the Indian scouts, to show that orders had been obeyed to the very letter, cut off the heads of all and carried these back with them as evidence.

On October 26, 1861, Governor Gilpin stated that "the core of the Rebellion" in Colorado "has at present withdrawn, to gather strength," particularly in Texas and from the Indian tribes in the Indian territory, with the view of returning to overwhelm opposition to itself among the loyal citizens. But those who formed the "core" did not return.

The two companies of Colorado volunteers sent to the assistance of Colonel Canby in New Mexico, in response to his appeal made toward the close of the year 1861, as mentioned on a preceding page, were the first organizations to leave Colorado for service in the war for the Union. They were familiary known in the territory at that time as "Captain 'Jim' Ford's Independent Company" and "Captain Dodd's Independent Company," both of which were recruited in and around Cañon City, which became their rendezvous. On August 29, 1861, Governor Gilpin authorized James H. Ford to raise a company of infantry, of which he appointed him captain. This was the beginning of the Second regiment of Colorado Volunteers, the later organization of which the governor then had in mind. The next day he appointed Alexander W. Robb first lieutenant and Cyrus H. DeForrest, Jr., second lieutenant of the company. On August 30th Theodore H. Dodd was appointed first lieutenant of another company, and soon afterward began at Cañon City to enlist men for it. Recruiting for these organizations proceeded

Captain James H. Ford.
(From a war-time photograph in the State Historical and Natural History Society's collection.)

through the autumn of 1861, and by December the ranks of both were filled.

Dodd's company left Cañon City December 7th, and marched to Fort Garland, in the San Luis valley, Colorado, by way of the Sangré dé Cristo pass, a distance of 110 miles, and at that fort, on December 14th, was mustered into the United States service for three years, with Dodd as its captain. One entry in the military records of that period mentions it as an "independent company of foot Volunteers," but in another it is provisionally designated as Company A of the Second Colorado Infantry. On December 27th Joseph C. W. Hall became second lieutenant; the records, so far as there are any on file in the Colorado capitol, being silent as to the first lieutenant.

Ford's company set out from Cañon City on December 12th for Fort Garland, where it arrived on the 21st, and was mustered in for three years' service on the 24th of that month, provisionally as Company B, Second Colorado Infantry, its officers being those commissioned by Governor Gilpin near the close of the previous August.

Captain Theodore H. Dodd.
(From a war-time photograph in the State Historical and Natural History Society's Collection.)

Captain Dodd's "foot Volunters" were hurried to Santa Fé, and after a few days in camp there put out, with other troops, on the long march down the Rio Grandé valley to Fort Craig, where they joined Colonel Canby's forces in time to participate in the hot battle of Valverdé, on February 21, 1862, in which they acquitted themselves gallantly.

Captain Ford's company remained at Fort Garland until February 4, 1862, when it started for Santa Fé, where it arrived on March 4th, having to break a roadway through deep snow a great part of the distance. On March 5th it left Santa Fé for Fort Union, to strengthen the small garrison at that post, where it arrived on March 11th.

In September and the fore part of October, 1861, two companies of home guards were organized in Denver City for six months' service, and were designated No. 1 and No. 2. Of Company 1 Joseph Ziegelmuller was appointed captain; Jacob Garres, first lieutenant, and William Wise, second lieutenant, by Governor Gilpin, late in August. Of Company 2 the governor, about the middle of September, appointed James W. Iddings, captain; John A. Latta, first lieutenant, and Adamson T. Dayton, second lieutenant. These organizations performed duty in Denver City and at Camp Weld.

They were recognized by the war department, duly paid for their services, and mustered out in the spring of 1862.

But the great military undertaking of Governor Gilpin and the loyal people of the territory, in the summer and autumn of 1861, was that of enlisting and getting into shape the very stalwart body of men known as the First regiment of Colorado Volunteer Infantry, an organization which finally arrested and hopelessly crushed, almost entirely by its own valor and strategy, the Confederate campaign in New Mexico. Early in the summer offers had been made from Colorado to the secretary of war to furnish immediately several companies, either of infantry or of cavalry, composed of "men inured to toil and hardship," but were ignobly repelled by the war department. Notwithstanding the feeling of disappointment caused by this rebuff from the general government, Governor Gilpin and other patriotic Colorado men resolved to organize a full regiment of infantry. The governor's direct authority from Washington for doing so, if any he obtained, is surrounded by much obscurity. But this does not matter now.

A movement was started in July by Samuel H. Cook and two associates in the South Clear Creek Mining District to raise a mounted company for service under General "Jim" Lane in Kansas. Cook soon succeeded in filling his company, but the governor persuaded him and his men to remain in the territory and join the new regiment. Authority to enlist other companies had been given to eager applicants, and recruiting offices opened in Denver City, in the Clear Creek mining towns, at Boulder City, Colorado City, and at several other places. A military camp, named "Camp Weld," in honor of Territorial Secretary Lewis L. Weld, was established on the Platte river, about two miles above what there then was of Denver City. Its locality is just west of the present artificial body of water called "Lake Archer." Here, at a cost of about $40,000, "comfortable and sufficient barracks" were constructed for the troops, and as the companies were formed they went into quarters there. By the first of October the ranks of most of the companies were completely filled.

Colonel John P. Slough, of the First Colorado Regiment.
(From a war-time photograph loaned by Mr. Samuel C.
Dorsey, of Denver.)
Colonel Slough resigned in April, 1862.

Appointments of company recruiting officers had been made in July and in the earlier part of August, and near the close of the last named month the principal regimental officers and most of the company officers were commissioned by Governor Gilpin, a majority of the commissions being dated August 26th. John P. Slough, a prominent lawyer of Denver City and recruiting captain of Company A, which he had enlisted in that town, was made colonel. Born and reared in Cincinnati, Ohio, he had been a member of the legislature of his native state, and secretary of the Ohio Democratic state central committee. While not an ideal military leader, he was a very capable man. Samuel F. Tappan, who as captain had recruited Company B at Central City and Black Hawk, was appointed lieutenant-colonel. To John M. Chivington, presiding elder of the Rocky Mountain district of the Methodist Episcopal church, the place of chaplain was tendered, but as he insisted upon having a strictly fighting position, and was enthusiastically for the Union, he was made major of the regiment—a most fortunate appointment. Later (November 1st) Rev. J. H. Kehler, of the Protestant Episcopal church, accepted the chaplaincy. On September 14th Dr. John F. Hamilton was appointed surgeon and Dr. Lewis C. Tolles assistant surgeon. About the middle of October the positions of quartermaster and adjutant were filled by company officers as mentioned below.

The department of the adjutant-general of the state of Colorado inherited from the territorial period but few records of the Colorado military organizations that served in the Civil War, nearly all of those which it now possesses being copies, secured by virtue of perseverance, of such as were available in the war department at Washington. But these, beside being confused and even contradictory in various details, and deficient as to important particulars, such as the names of the killed and the wounded, are far from complete in series. However, in the following we have, according to the scattered data in these records, the names and rank of the original company officers, together with the changes made among them when the regimental officers were appointed, as well as other changes up to the time when the organization marched forth upon its victorious campaign in New Mexico:

Company A—John P. Slough, captain; James R. Shaffer, first lieutenant; Edward W. Wynkoop, second lieutenant. When Captain Slough was appointed colonel, Lieutenant Wynkoop was promoted captain of the company, and Joseph C. Davidson, who had been first sergeant of Company C, succeeded Wynkoop as second lieutenant of Company A. The regimental roster states that Davidson was "appointed adjutant October 18, 1861," while the pay roll of January 1, 1862, has him serving as second lieutenant of this company. Probably he was detailed to act as adjutant, instead of being "appointed." On February 7, 1862, Davidson was promoted first lieutenant and transferred to Company E to succeed Lieutenant Buell, deceased. The records do not show who succeeded him at that time as second lieutenant of Company A.

Dr. John F. Hamilton, Surgeon of the First Colorado Regiment.
(From a war-time photograph loaned by Mr. Samuel C. Dorsey, of Denver.)

Company B—Samuel F. Tappan, captain; Isaac Gray, first lieutenant; Edward A. Jacobs, second lieutenant. When Captain Tappan was appointed lieutenant-colonel, Samuel M. Logan, who appears to have been an "unattached" first lieutenant since July 27th, was commissioned captain of the company.

Company C—Richard Sopris, captain; Alfred S. Cobb, first lieutenant; Clark Chambers, second lieutenant. Most of the men of this company were enlisted at Denver City and in the Buckskin Joe mining district.

Company D—Jacob Downing, captain; William F. Roath, first lieutenant; Eli Dickerson, second lieutenant. This company was recruited principally at Denver City.

Company E—Scott J. Anthony, captain; Julius O. Buell, first lieutenant; James A. Dawson, second lieutenant. Buell died at Camp Weld on February 6, 1862—the first death among the officers—and was succeeded by Joseph C. Davidson, former second lieutenant of Company A. Chiefly, the company was enlisted in the mining towns of Oro City and Laurett and in their vicinity.

Company F—Samuel H. Cook, captain; George Nelson, first lieutenant; William F. Marshall, second lieutenant. Recruited in the South Clear Creek mining district.

Company G—Josiah W. Hambleton, captain; William F. Wilder, first lieutenant; John C. Anderson, second lieutenant. On November 30, 1861, Captain Hambleton was cashiered by court martial for insubordination. First Lieutenant Wilder then was promoted captain of the company; Second Lieutenant Anderson, who had been serving as quartermaster of the regiment since October 14th, was promoted first lieutenant, and First Sergeant George H. Hardin was promoted second lieutenant to succeed Anderson. Later (in July, 1862) Captain Hambleton was given an honorable discharge, and enlisted in the Third regiment of Colorado Volunteers, of one of the companies of which he was subsequently appointed second lieutenant. Nearly all of the enlistments in this company were made at Nevada, Empire City and neighboring Clear Creek mining camps.

Company H—George L. Sanborn, captain; Jacob P. Bonesteel, first lieutenant; Byron N. Sanford, second lieutenant. This company, which was originally intended by Captain Sanborn to be of the "Zouave" order, and to be taken to the states, was recruited mainly at Central City.

Company I—Charles Mailie, captain; Charles Kerber, first lieutenant; John Baker, second lieutenant. The company consisted mostly of Germans, and was enlisted in Denver City, and in Central City and other towns in the Clear Creek mining districts.

Company K—Charles P. Marion, captain; George S. Eayers, first lieutenant; Robert McDonald, second lieutenant. Captain Marion was cashiered on November 30, 1861, for insubordination, Samuel H. Robbins being commissioned to succeed him. Lieutenant Eay-

4

ers then resigned, and Silas S. Soulé was appointed as his successor. Lieutenant Eayers afterward became first lieutenant of McLain's famous Colorado battery. Most of the men of this company hailed from Central City and Denver.

On December 18th George L. Shoup was appointed second lieutenant, and appears to have been assigned to duty on Colonel Slough's staff. A decade or so ago he was elected United States senator from the state of Idaho. On February 11, 1862, Charles C. Hawley, who also figures as one of Colonel Slough's staff officers, was appointed second lieutenant.

The material of the regiment probably was as good as any that ever was brought together in a military organization. The men were uncommonly hardy and well seasoned, and not in the habit of being afraid. The average height of those of Company A, which may be taken as a representative unit of the regiment, was 5 feet 8½ inches, the tallest being 6 feet 3¼ inches. The "cosmopolitan" character of the population of the territory of Colorado at that time was reflected in the nativity of the members of the same company when it was mustered into the service: New York, 17; Ohio, 9; Vermont, 5; Pennsylvania, 4; Illinois, 3; Virginia, Indiana and New Jersey, each 2; Maine, Maryland, Massachusetts, Rhode Island, Michigan, Missouri and Iowa, each 1; Ireland, 7; Canada, 6; Scotland, 4; Germany and England, each 2; Wales, 1.

Late in the autumn three companies of the regiment were sent to Fort Wise (afterward renamed "Fort Lyon," in honor of General Nathaniel Lyon, the Federal commander who was killed in the battle of Wilson's Creek, Missouri), on the Arkansas river, more than two hundred miles southeast of Denver City, under the command of Lieutenant-Colonel Tappan, to garrison that post, the other companies remaining in quarters at Camp Weld, of which Major Chivington had been placed in immediate charge.

This stout-hearted soldier, John Milton Chivington, was born January 27, 1821, near Lebanon, Ohio. His father was an Irishman and his mother was of Scotch descent, both of whom lived near Lexington, Kentucky. Soon after their marriage they removed to Warren county, Ohio. The father had been a soldier

Major John M. Chivington, of the First Colorado Regiment.
(From a war-time photograph in the State Historical and Natural History Society's
Collection.)
Major Chivington was promoted Colonel of the Regiment in April, 1862.

under General William Henry Harrison in the War of 1812, with
England, and fought with him, October 5, 1813, in the Battle of
the Thames, in Canada. The son had inherited the martial spirit
of his father, and was, as often remarked by his friends, "a born
fighter." In addition, he was a staunch antagonist to human slavery. He joined in 1848 the conference of the Methodist Episcopal
Church at Pleasant Green, Cooper county, Missouri, and was ordained a preacher. He delivered his first sermon in Quincy, Illinois,
and thereafter was engaged in church work in Illinois, Missouri and
Nebraska—exhibiting wonderful power in the camp meetings of
his denomination—until he removed to Denver City in 1860. During the four next preceding years he had served as a presiding elder
in Nebraska, having his residence part of the time in Omaha and
part in Nebraska City. He came to Colorado as presiding elder of
the Rocky Mountain district, a church office which he was filling
acceptably at the time the First regiment of Colorado Volunteers
was organized. He left Colorado a few years after the Civil War,
and resided in California and in Ohio until 1883, when he returned
to Denver, where he remained the rest of his days, his death occurring on October 4, 1894. His brother, Lewis Chivington, a gallant
colonel in the Confederate army, was killed August 10, 1861, in the
bloody battle of Wilson's Creek.

Chivington developed extraordinary military ability, although he
had had no military training before he abandoned the pulpit for the
battlefield. In action he became the incarnation of war. The brav-
est of the brave, a giant in stature, and a whirlwind in strife, he
had, also, the rather unusual qualities that go to make soldiers personally love such a leader and eager to follow him into the jaws of
death. The admiration and devotion of his men became unbounded.
He was their ideal of a dashing, fearless, fighting commander.

Now a few words concerning the transactions which led to Governor Gilpin's removal from his position as chief executive of the
territory of Colorado. During the summer and autumn of 1861,
when the enlistment of the First regiment of Colorado Volunteers
and of the two independent companies was under way, and also
during a large part of the time in which these troops remained

in Colorado inactive, the treasury of the territory was practically without money for military purposes. The Washington government had placed no war fund at the governor's disposal, nor had it conferred upon him any authority to create indebtedness on Federal account. To organize and maintain, even for a short period, such a number of soldiers requires the expenditure of a comparatively large sum of money. As the territory was without ready means with which to make such expenditures, the governor met the emergency with a method that he believed to be proper and justified. In payment of incidental expenses and for general military supplies he issued negotiable drafts directly upon the national treasury at Washington, for which he had no legal authority. These drafts were willingly accepted by those to whom money was due on military account, and some of them passed from hand to hand in Colorado as currency, upon the presumption that they were valid documents, which would be paid without question when they finally reached Washington. The sum of such drafts issued by the governor was about $375,000.

When these issues appeared at Washington they were repudiated by the treasury department and went to protest. The effect of this was ruinous to merchants and many others in Colorado who had assisted in organizing and maintaining the troops. Governor Gilpin's situation may be imagined. A bitter public sentiment arose against him, and he was assailed upon every hand by exasperated holders of his drafts. As an old army officer he was held to have known the government's rigid financial methods, and it was principally because of his presumed knowledge of such matters that the people had unquestioningly accepted his irregular and illegal orders upon the national treasury. He declared that he had been personally assured by men high in authority in Washington that this irregular method would be recognized in the emergency and that his drafts would be honored, and there is no reason to doubt that he had been given some such assurance. However, there was a storm at Washington over the matter, which the governor endeavored to allay, and to secure payment of the drafts, by going there and stating the conditions existing in Colorado. But in this he was unsuc-

View of Denver City in the Civil War Period.

(From a lithograph of a drawing made by Albert E. Matthews in 1865, in the collection of early views in Colorado of Mr. Charles R. Dudley, of Denver. Between the beginning and the close of the war the town made very slow progress, and its general appearance was but little changed.)

cessful. The affair finally became one for cabinet consideration. and the result of this was that John Evans, of Illinois, came to Colorado in May, 1862, as Gilpin's successor—within two months after the regiment which had been chiefly the indirect cause of the trouble had defeated the Confederates at La Gloriéta, and practically ended their operations in New Mexico.

Later a large part of the indebtedness was paid by the Washington government. Original holders of Governor Gilpin's paper, who could prepare itemized and verified accounts of their claims for which drafts had been issued in payment, succeeded in getting their money after more or less delay. But the drafts, as such, were not recognized in any manner by the treasury department, and every one of them which had passed from original hands and could not successfully be thrown back upon the person to whom it had been issued became a total loss to the holder. Much of the paper was rendered worthless by payees, who had passed it to others, becoming scattered, many of them having left the territory before the government began to adjust and pay any of the claims.

But no one questioned Governor Gilpin's integrity, the purity of his purpose, or the sincerity of his zeal to protect the people from invasion, and to serve them to the best of his ability. He was in some ways a "visionary" man, whose mind and thoughts occasionally were far above the practical affairs of every-day life, and his enthusiasm for the Union overshadowed all other things. Notwithstanding the unfortunate consequences of his method of financing his military preparations, the people, not only those of Colorado, but of the country at large, were immeasurably indebted to him for the promptness, vigor and earnestness with which he made ready for war.

GENERAL SIBLEY'S MOVEMENT UP THE RIO GRANDÉ VALLEY.

It has already been mentioned that General Sibley arrived at Fort Bliss, Texas, near the close of the year 1861, and then took personal command of the forces he had raised for the consummation of the Confederate purposes in the Southwest, New Mexico having been claimed as already belonging to the Southern Confederacy. On the 11th of January, 1862, he was still detained at this fort, but the main portion of his brigade had crossed the boundary line between Texas and New Mexico some three weeks before, and was encamped in the Mésilla valley, thirty miles to the north. In the succeeding five days he had joined these troops and was conducting their march to Fort Thorn, forty miles farther up the Rio Grandé, where he remained with them until the fore part of February. Thus nearly two months had been lost in waiting for belated reenforcements from San Antonio to reach him. During that time he was engaged in completing arrangements to have the orders of President Davis executed in securing a regiment of natives by enlistment and conscription. He sent a detachment of his small army to Tucson, two hundred and fifty miles to the west, to hold the western part of New Mexico for the Confederacy and to sustain the authority of Colonel John R. Baylor, its military governor, and which arrived there on February 28th. He dispatched one of his officers, Colonel James Reily, as an envoy to the chief executive of the state of Chihuahua in Mexico, to whom was delivered a communication from him, and from whom he received a satisfactory response. According to General Sibley's report, "friendship and good will" were pledged by one to the other, and a treaty formed to "establish friendly relations" between their respective governments. The governor declared that "he would not permit Federal troops to pass through his territory to invade Texas;" that he would not officially sanction the occupancy of any part of it "by foreign troops;" that he would not prevent the purchase of supplies in his state by any one in the Texan expedition, and that, whenever necessary, he would afford protection to the persons and property of the citizens of the Confederacy. Colonel Reily boastfully congratulated his general "on having obtained the first official recognition of the government of the Southern States" by any foreign power. He proceeded afterward with an escort on a similar mission to the state of Sonora in Mexico, but was reported to have secured from its chief executive only the privilege "of buying for cash anything" its people had to sell.

Fort Thorn.
(From a wood engraving in "El Gringo," by W. W. H. Davis, 1857.)

On the 7th of February General Sibley set out from Fort Thorn with about 3,000 men, fifteen pieces of artillery, and a long and heavy supply train, upon his march up the valley of the Rio Grandé, on the west side of the river, and on the 12th of that month he was in camp at a point seven miles below Fort Craig. Four days afterward he offered battle on an open plain within two miles of the post, to its garrison under Colonel Canby, who declined the challenge, as he hoped to select a position more advantageous to himself, and because his troops, especially his New Mexico volunteers, were, he feared, much less effective on an open battlefield. The Texans withdrew down the valley on the 19th of February, and at their former camp crossed the river to its east bank. To pass the fort on their left beyond the range of its guns, and to arrive at the upper ford in the river, twelve miles above and five from Fort Craig, where they could compel the Federals to meet them in a general engagement, they moved northward on the following day over extremely rough ground, and made a "dry camp" late in the afternoon in a pine grove between ridges of malpais rock, near the ends of immense volcanic overflows from at least two craters thirty to forty miles to the eastward. Owing to ridges in the overflows, some of them sixty feet in height, between the camp and the river, it was impossible for the troops at the fort, with their cavalry and artillery, to reach the Confederates in their camp, which was about two miles directly to the east, and so only feeble efforts could be made to interrupt, much less to prevent, their march to the upper ford.

This crossing was near an old hamlet called Valverdé, and is now bordered on the west by the town of San Marcial. Valverdé is somewhat famous in the early, as well as in the later, history of the valley. Expeditions along the Rio Grandé often halted here to rest and to plan their future operations. They found here large groves of pine and cottonwood, particularly on the east side of the stream, and an easy access to water for themselves and their animals. Here the Army of the West, under General Kearny, after taking possession of New Mexico, met late in 1846 the celebrated scout, Kit Carson, who had brought from southern California an express stating that Colonel Frémont and Commodore Stockton had received the surrender of that country, and that the American flag was floating in every part of it. Kearny's army was here divided, one portion proceeding under Colonel Doniphan down the valley on its way to Chihuahua in Mexico, and the other, under General Kearny, to southern California, with Carson returning as the guide.

At Valverdé, on February 21, 1862, occurred the first severe engagement between the Union and the Confederate forces in the Southwest, and, considering the comparatively small number of troops engaged, it was a desperate encounter. The day was a

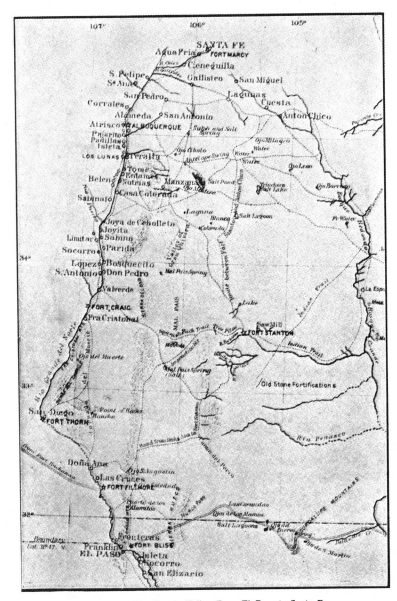

Map of the Rio Grande Valley From El Paso to Santa Fe.
(From a Military Map issued by the War Department in 1857, in the State Historical
and Natural History Society's collection.)

typical one of early spring in New Mexico, with a clear sky and a cool and bracing atmosphere. The battlefield terminated on the south in the Mésa de la Contadéra, which, composed of sandrock covered by lava, rises over three hundred feet abruptly from the river and the plain, and extends easterly three miles. Rows of small hills and sand ridges run, not far back from the river, northward over a mile to another, but lower, mésa. A grove or bosqué of large cottonwood trees, with openings between them, filled a considerable part of this area.

Early in the morning the Texans left their camp opposite Fort Craig, and went in detachments during the forenoon onto the battlefield from the rear, and descended the slope to the river bottoms. Their immediate object was to find water for their horses and mules, which had been without any for twenty-four hours. They purposed, also, to ford the stream here and continue their march up the valley on its west side. Opposition to their movement was expected from troops at the fort, and so from their camp they made a demonstration to attack it before noon, to prevent, if possible, any considerable body of its garrison leaving for the ford. In this attempt they were disappointed. But they succeeded in alarming a regiment of militia, raised in New Mexico, which fled from the place, and could not then or afterward be brought into the engagement.

Of the numerical strength of the two armies Colonel Canby, in his report to the adjutant-general of the army at Washington, said:

"His [Sibley's] force consisted of Riley's and Green's regiments, five companies of Steele's and five of Baylor's regiments, Teel's and Riley's batteries, and three independent companies, making a nominal aggregate, as indicated by captured rolls and returns, of nearly 3,000 men, but reduced, it was understood, by sickness and detachments to about 2,600 when it reached this neighborhood.

"To oppose this force I had concentrated at this post [Fort Craig] five companies of the Fifth, three of the Seventh and three of the Tenth Infantry, two companies of the First and five of the Third Cavalry, McRae's battery (G of the Second and I of the Third Cavalry), and a company of Colorado volunteers [Dodd's]. The New Mexican troops consisted of the First Regiment (Carson's), seven companies of the Second, seven of the Third, one of the Fourth, two of the Fifth, Graydon's Spy-Company, and about 1,000 hastily-collected and unorganized militia, making on the morning of the 21st an aggregate present of 3,810."

General Sibley was in immediate command of his army until early in the afternoon, when, on account of illness, he transferred it to Colonel Thomas Green, one of his most efficient officers. The Federal forces were, until the middle of the afternoon, under the full charge of Lieutenant-Colonel Benjamin S. Roberts, of the Third regiment United States Cavalry, and at the time colonel of the Fifth New Mexico Infantry. He was a gallant, trusted and able leader, who had refused, at the opening of the war, to join his associates in the United States army who were then stationed in New Mexico, and with them to enter the service of the Confederate government. Very largely through his influence most of the junior officers and nearly all of the private soldiers remained true to their government. Colonel Canby arrived on the ground from the fort late in the day, and assumed the entire direction of his men. It was the opinion of many of these that the

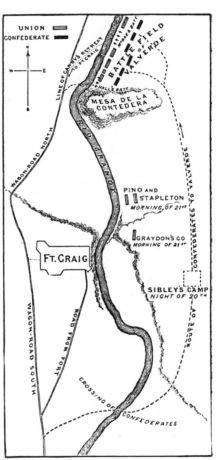

Map of the Fort Craig Locality, Showing the Relative Situation of the Battlefield of Valverde to the Fort.
(From "Battles and Leaders of the Civil War." The Century Company, 1887.)

final result of the battle would have been different if Colonel Roberts had retained the charge to the end. The contest began about nine o'clock in the morning and lasted until near sunset, while the severest fighting was done just before noon and near the close of the afternoon. On both sides artillery in the least number, infantry in the largest and cavalry in an intermediate were engaged. During the day the action was conducted principally by the first-named branch, using field pieces and mountain howitzers, under the orders of Major Trevanion T. Teel and Lieutenant John Riley of the Confederates, and under those of Captain Alexander McRae and Lieutenant Robert H. Hall of the Federals. McRae's battery was a provisional one, manned, not by regular artillerymen, but by men of Company G of the Second and of Company I of the Third Regular Cavalry, Captain McRae being an officer of the last-named regiment.

Operations started with fierce cannonading from both banks of the river, near the high mésa, where was the lower and principal crossing. The Union gunners, annoyed by the Texan sharpshooters hidden behind rocks and trees on the slopes of this mésa, were compelled to move their battery from a position directly across the stream from it to a point at the north, where they could still, at the very water's edge, defend this crossing, and fire their shots into the thick bosqué of cottonwoods on the opposite bank. Aided by infantry and dismounted cavalry of the regulars, who had forded the Rio Grandé, they succeeded by noon in driving the Confederates from the eastern river bottom among the cottonwoods back into an old dry channel of the stream and behind a long ridge of sand. This contest was, at times, very desperate. Three efforts were made by the enemy to regain the positions they had lost in the southern section of the battlefield, and once the Federal forces attempted to capture one of their batteries, which had been partially disabled. All these movements failed. Meanwhile the First regiment of New Mexico Volunteers, under the command of Colonel Kit Carson, was moved about a mile north on the western side of the river into a cottonwood grove, to prevent an attack of 500 Texan cavalry from that direction.

Nearly all of the Union troops were ordered early in the afternoon across the stream. Lieutenant Hall's two 24-pounder howitzers, with their supports, were placed in the southern portion of the field, which had been occupied in the morning by the Confederates. Captain McRae's six splendid field pieces, with an inadequate support, were stationed three-fourths of a mile northward, near the upper crossing. The Texans, on retreating to the old channel above

Lieutenant-Colonel William R. Scurry, the Battle-Leader
of the Confederate Forces in New Mexico in 1862.
(From a war-time photograph in the State Historical and
Natural History Society's collection.)

mentioned, had extended their right up the same to points opposite and beyond the latter battery and behind some sand hills. The remainder of the afternoon was occupied by both armies in desultory firing at each other, mainly by their artillery, and in disposing of their forces for the final and decisive struggle that occurred an hour before sundown. An episode was brought about in the northern extremity of the field by a company of the Texan cavalry, armed with lances, dashing against Captain Dodd's company of Colorado volunteers, formed into a hollow square. The Texans were quickly repulsed, many of them being tumbled out of their saddles in a few minutes. These Colorado volunteers, under fire for the first time, fought like seasoned veterans. According to Colonel Canby's final report, the killed and the wounded of the company numbered thirty, a greater number of casualties than that of any other organization of an equal number of men engaged in the battle. It would seem that the colonel was trying the mettle of the first Colorado soldiers he had seen.

Colonel Canby, on assuming full charge of the Federal forces, decided at once to strengthen the right wing of his little army, and, if possible, to flank the enemy's left, dissolving it or doubling it back upon its right, fronting McRae's battery. Colonel Carson's regiment was added to the detachment of regulars supporting Hall's mountain howitzers, in position almost in the shadow of the high mésa to the south. Chiefly other volunteers were assigned to the defense of the field pieces in the northern wing. Five companies of the Second regiment of New Mexico Volunteers, under Colonel Miguel E. Pino (himself a brave and gallant officer). refused to obey the order to cross the river from the west side and aid in this defense.

The Confederates, discovering the arrangements made for the Federal right wing, placed Major Henry W. Raguet in command of their extreme left, and supplied him with a sufficient force to check temporarily the advance of Canby's right. While doing this they concentrated the larger portion of their army in the opposite direction, concealed behind the sand hills, for the purpose of assaulting the weakened end of the Union line. In a furious attempt of the Texans to capture Lieutenant Hall's guns, Colonel Carson's regiment did effectual service in resisting and driving back Major Raguet's detachments. He was said to have shot, with his own hand, several of his men who, from cowardice, attempted to desert the ranks by taking to their heels. When the contest here was at its height, the Texans under cover at the other extremity of the field leaped, at a given signal, upon the sand ridges in their front, armed with rifles, double-barreled shot guns, pistols and *machetes*, and rushed in headlong confusion about 700 yards down the slope, through a storm of grape shot and canister from McRae's little band of heroes, and around his battery, which they seized within eight minutes, after killing or severely wounding about fifteen of

the ninety-three regulars working these guns. They were directed and cheered from the rear in this onslaught by Lieutenant-Colonel William R. Scurry, whose clarion voice was heard above the yells, shouts and hurrahs of the charging party and of the roar of the artillery. These men were led by Major S. A. Lockridge, whose death at the very muzzle of one of the cannon was greatly lamented by his comrades. Captain McRae, the battery's commander, also was slain. It was told that a Texan officer in the attack shouted

Major Trevanion T. Teel, Commander of General Sibley's Artillery.
(From an after-the-war photograph in the State Historical and Natural History Society's collection.)

to him: "Surrender, McRae! we don't want to kill you!" and that from him, with his right arm shattered by a bullet, and leaning upon one of his pieces, came the instantaneous response: "I shall never forsake my guns!" At that moment both he and Major Lockridge were instantly killed, and their bodies fell limp across the gun and their blood flowed upon its surface. The brave, loyal and accomplished McRae had won the truest esteem and admiration of his fellow-soldiers. His commander said of him: "He died, as he had lived, an example of the best and highest qualities that man can possess." He belonged to a distinguished family in the South, having been born in North Carolina, and had heroically resisted the importunities of his relatives to abandon the cause of the Union, and those of Southern leaders to join his fortunes with the Confederacy.

Had the battery been efficiently supported by the troops at hand it would not have been taken. Henry Connelly, governor of New Mexico, in reporting this affair to the secretary of state, at Washington, from Santa Fé, under date of March 1st, said:

"It is painful to relate that of the forces in position for the protection of the battery not one company advanced to its relief or even fired upon the enemy as he approached. The force consisted of two or more companies of regular troops and one regiment of New Mexico volunteers. The regulars were ordered—nay, implored—to charge the enemy, by Colonel Canby, Major Donaldson and Colonel Collins, superintendent of Indian affairs, who were all three present, in immediate contact with the troops and within 10 or 20 yards of the battery when it was taken. The regulars having refused to advance, the volunteers followed their example, and both retired from the field, recrossing the river and leaving the battery in possession of the enemy."

Captain Gurden Chapin, of the Seventh United States Infantry, and a member of Colonel Canby's staff, stated in one of his reports that his commander "beseeched and begged, ordered and imperatively commanded, the troops to save his guns, and a deaf ear met alike his supplications and commands." Refusal on the part of these, and of the others of his troops which have been mentioned, to obey orders, was reported by Colonel Canby to Washington as the "immediate cause of the disaster" that befell his army at Valverdé. Major James L. Donaldson, in a report to the adjutant-general of the army, at Washington, said of the New Mexico volunteers: "They have a traditionary fear of the Texans, and will not face them in the field."

The assaulting Confederates soon were in full possession of McRae's battery. Colonel Canby, whose horse was shot under him, perceived, after the loss of these guns, that further contest was futile, and at once ordered all of his troops who were still on the east side of the Rio Grandé to recross the stream and return to the fort. The lost battery and that of Major Teel were then quickly brought into action by the Confederates to hasten the retreat of the Union forces, which Colonel Canby finally accomplished with only a slight loss of men and munitions of war.

In proportion to the number of the troops actually engaged in the fight, the losses in killed and wounded on the Union side were unusually heavy. Colonel Roberts said in his report that "they were unexampled, it is believed, in any single battle ever fought on this continent." The casualties were confined almost entirely to the regulars and to Dodd's company of Colorado volunteers, about one-third of the men of the latter having been struck. Reports of the Union losses are somewhat at variance. Captain Chapin stated on February 28th that "our loss, so far as ascertained up to the present moment, is sixty-two killed and about 140 wounded." According to Colonel's Canby's report he had three officers and sixty-five enlisted men killed on the field; three officers and 157 enlisted men wounded, of whom "a number died" soon afterward, and one officer and thirty-four enlisted men missing, a total of 263. Dr. Basil Norris, assistant surgeon, United States army, in charge of the hospitals at Fort Craig, reporting from that post on March 5th to his superior, Dr. E. I. Baily, surgeon, United States army, and medical director of the Department of New Mexico, at Santa Fé, stated that "fifty-six men were killed on the field, including nine volunteers; 147 men were brought to the hospitals wounded, seventeen of whom have since died." Nothing very definite can be ascertained as to General Sibley's losses. He reported forty of his men killed, including two officers, and thought 100 would cover the number of his wounded. But it appears to have been his policy to minimize every misfortune that befell him. Colonel Thomas Green reported forty-one dead and 150 wounded. Governor Connelly, in a communication to Washington, said: "The loss of the enemy, it is ascertained by deserters from their camp, was very large—at least 300 killed, and the wounded in proportion." However, deserters usually are not good authorities. Captain Chapin reported the Confederate loss at "150 killed and 450 wounded." Probably the facts lie somewhere about midway between the figures of General Sibley and those of Captain Chapin. The Confederate dead were buried together on the battlefield, and those of the Union forces at Fort Craig, with military honors.

On the morrow General Sibley, in the flush of his victory, sent, under a flag of truce, three of his officers to Colonel Canby, who were instructed to demand the immediate surrender of the fort, which demand was promptly rejected. The first of these officers was the Lieutenant-Colonel Scurry, already mentioned; the second,

Colonel Christopher ("Kit") Carson.
(From a wood engraving supplied by the author.)

Lieutenant Tom P. Ochiltree, afterward governor of Texas and a member of the United States congress, the third being Captain D. W. Shannon, who was taken prisoner in a subsequent battle in the territory. It was reported, but not confirmed, that this commission regarded the fort as too strongly defended to be taken by assault or siege at the time. Also, that they were deceived as to the number and calibre of the real cannon mounted on its bastions, for while some of these were metal, the others were said to be large-size wooden ones—mere Quaker guns.

Colonel Canby, though depressed in spirit by his defeat, resolved still to make all efforts possible with his command to thwart the purpose of the Texans to acquire possession of the Southwest and thus to separate the Pacific Coast from the Union. Subsequent events will show to what extent he succeeded in this determination through his own efforts. At Santa Fé, at that time, the belief that he could be successful with his small number of trustworthy troops was by no means sanguine. The territory's capital turned toward Colorado for help. Captain Gurden Chapin, acting inspector-general at the time, in a report to Major-General H. W. Halleck, at St. Louis, from Santa Fé, on February 28th, said:

"* * * It is needless to say that this country is in a critical condition. The militia have all run away and the New Mexican volunteers are deserting in large numbers. No dependence whatever can be placed on the natives; they are worse than worthless; they are really aids to the enemy, who catch them, take their arms and tell them to go home.

"A force of Colorado volunteers is already on the way to assist us, and they may possibly arrive in time to save us from immediate danger; * * *."

Brevet-Captain George H. Pettis, who was adjutant of the First New Mexico Volunteer Infantry, in his *Confederate Invasion of New Mexico and Arizona* (a short chapter in *Battles and Leaders of the Civil War:* The Century Company, 1888), records the following amusing incident that occurred the night before the battle of Valverdé, and which shows how tragedy and comedy may go hand in hand in a time of war:

"Captain James Graydon (familiarly known as 'Paddy' Graydon) had been a soldier in the regular army, and on the approach of the Confederates had been authorized to organize an independent spy company, and as such it was mustered into the service of the United States. As its name implies, it was truly an 'independent' company. It was seldom under the restraint of a superior officer, as it was nearly all the time on the road, its captain not liking the monotony of garrison life. Captain Graydon was a brave man, and no undertaking was too hazardous for him to attempt. His company were nearly all natives of New Mexico, and they would go anywhere their captain would lead them. On the evening of February 20th, when the enemy were encamped opposite Fort Craig. Graydon was allowed to make a night attack upon them. Without explaining the details of his plan he had prepared a couple of wooden boxes, in each of which half a dozen 24-pounder howitzer shells were placed, with the fuses cut. These boxes were securely lashed on the backs of two old mules, and the captain, with three or four of his men, crossed the river just below the fort and proceeded in the darkness toward the Confederate camp. Graydon's project was to get the torpedo mules within sight of the enemy's picket line without being discovered, when he was to light the fuses, and the mules, being directed toward the picket line, would move in the direction of the animals there. He finally arrived within 150 yards of the picket line, and, everything being in readiness, the fuses of the boxes were fired, and the captain and his party commenced their retreat, when to their consternation they found that the mules, instead of going toward the enemy, were following themselves; the shells soon began to explode, the Confederate camp was quickly under arms, and Graydon's party made its way back to Fort Craig without the mules."

Central and Northern Parts of the Battlefield of Valverde.   From the West Side of the
Rio Grande.
(From one of the author's photographs.)
The picture on the opposite page is a continuation, to the right, of this view.

The Confederate troops remained in camp, a mile and a quarter to the east of the Valverdé battleground, the succeeding two days, burying their dead and arranging to carry their wounded to Socorro, a distance of twenty-five miles. At Socorro they decided to push rapidly forward along the river to the larger towns, where provisions, in the shape of "breadstuff and meat," could be obtained, and where they could deprive Colonel Canby of "all communication with his supplies." All of their own rations on hand would last them scarcely five days, and subsistence of any kind could not be procured in the region below, where they had operated for some

months, as it had been wholly consumed by them. By March 2d
their advance guard was in the vicinity of Albuquerqué, when the
small force of Federal troops stationed there hurriedly left for
Santa Fé, first destroying nearly all of the army stores that it could
not convey away with teams. On the third day afterward, it, with
another force at the capital of the territory, abandoned that city
for Fort Union, transporting in 120 wagons the most valuable government supplies in their charge, worth a quarter of a million dol-

Southern End of the Battlefield of Valverde.   From the West Side of the Rio Grande.
(From one of the author's photographs.)
This is a continuation, to the right, of the view on the opposite page.

lars. They arrived safely at their destination on the 10th of that
month, where they found adequate protection. The posts evacuated
by them were very soon occupied by a strong advance guard of the
invaders, whose main body did not reach Albuquerqué until the 17th
of March.

On the way from Valverdé none of the Confederate detachments
met with any further resistance, and yet they were sorely disappointed by the cool, if not hostile, reception given them by a large
number of the people. As a retaliation they exacted money from
wealthy New Mexicans who had not escaped from the valley at

their approach, and confiscated property belonging to families known to favor the Federal cause. Two of the Armijo brothers, positive sympathizers, placed their stores of merchandise, valued at $200,000, at the disposal of General Sibley's troops. Especially at Albuquerqué, Santa Fé and Cubéro, seventy miles to the west of the Rio Grandé and eight beyond the Laguna Pueblo, all available commissary, forage and clothing supplies were seized by the Confederates; so a sufficient quantity of these necessaries for the army was

The Armijo Residence in Old Albuquerque.
(From one of the author's photographs.)

on hand to last it about three months. The decision was then formed to advance, as soon they could be ready, with their entire force, to Fort Union, ahead only four days' march, and, if possible, to capture it, with its great stores of military supplies, as the last remaining menace of importance to their full possession of the territory. Their confidence in their ability to demolish it with their artillery, by planting their larger guns on the hills to the west of it, suggests that perhaps General Sibley had not been informed of the recent construction there of an earthwork fortification that virtually had superseded the old post, with which the Confederate commander was familiar. He appears to have been entirely in the dark as to the advance from Colorado of a body of men destined to work his complete undoing.

Major Charles L. Pyron, with 500 mounted men, was sent forward from Albuquerqué to Santa Fé, with the purpose of leading the march. He had been a trusted officer under Colonel Baylor during the campaign of the preceding summer and fall in the Mésilla valley and its adjacent region, and had participated there in the masterful skirmishes with the Federal troops. He had creditably filled leading positions in the recent battle at Valverdé, being "in the thickest of the fray" in the decisive charge at its close.

"One of Sibley's Texas Rangers."
(From Lossing's "Pictorial History of the Civil War," 1868.)

The larger division of "Sibley's Brigade" was placed in charge of Lieutenant-Colonel Scurry, and was ordered to proceed, with the principal train of supplies, from Albuquerqué by way of Bernalillo to Galistéo, which is less than fifteen miles from the western end of La Gloriéta pass. Here he could be joined at the appropriate time by Pyron's battalion from Santa Fé. Colonel Scurry belonged to a distinguished family in Texas, which had emigrated from Tennessee and settled early in that state. He served as a district attorney in the period when it was a republic, and as a major in a Texas regiment under General Zachary Taylor in the Mexican War, gaining celebrity in the battle of Monterey. His name was signed February 8, 1861, to the declaration of the causes that impelled his state to secede from the

Federal Union, a sequel of an ordinance passed a week before at the capital by a convention to which he was a delegate. He was commissioned August 23d of the same year, by the Confederacy, as lieutenant-colonel of the Fourth regiment of Texas Mounted Infantry, and assigned to the command of General Sibley. At Valverdé he was recognized as the conspicuous Confederate hero in the battle. Upon his return home after the Rio Grandé campaign he was promoted brigadier-general.

The accompanying grotesque picture of "One of Sibley's Texas Rangers," from Lossing's *Pictorial History of the Civil War* (volume II, page 187), published in 1868, is said to have been made "from a sketch by one of Colonel Canby's subalterns." In a footnote the following description is given of this ferocious-looking being, who is so largely a product of imagination:

"These Rangers who went into the rebellion were described as being, many of them, a desperate set of fellows, having no higher motive than plunder and adventure. They were half savage, and each was mounted on a mustang horse. Each man carried a rifle, a tomahawk, a bowie knife, a pair of Colt's revolvers, and a lasso for catching and throwing the horses of a flying foe."

ADVANCE OF THE FIRST COLORADO REGIMENT INTO NEW MEXICO.

While the last preparations of the Confederates for a movement and an attack on Fort Union were being matured, the First regiment of Colorado Volunteers was on the march to counteract and defeat them. The men had remained in quarters, anxious and impatient, since the organization of the regiment. News of the entrance of General Sibley's army into the Rio Grandé valley reached Denver in the fore part of January, and efforts were made at once to obtain orders from Major-General David Hunter at Fort Leavenworth, Kansas, in command of the Department of Kansas, which included also the territory of Colorado, for the Colorado regiment immediately to go to the assistance of Colonel Canby. But more than a month elapsed before the command was given. On February 14th Secretary and Acting Governor Lewis L. Weld (Governor Gilpin being absent from the territory at the time) received from General Hunter the following:

"Headquarters, Department of Kansas,
"Fort Leavenworth, Kan., February 10, 1862.

"To His Excellency, Acting Governor of Colorado, Denver City, Colo.:

"Send all available forces you can possibly spare to reinforce Colonel Canby, commanding Department of New Mexico, and to keep open his communication through Fort Wise. Act promptly and with all the discretion of your latest information as to what may be necessary and where the troops of Colorado can do most service.
"D. HUNTER,
"Major-General, Commanding."

On the 22d of that month, the next day after the disastrous engagement at Valverdé, the companies of the regiment at Camp Weld, and on the 3d of March, following, the other companies, under the charge of Lieutenant-Colonel Tappan at Fort Wise, left their respective quarters for the scenes of active operations. Acting

Governor Weld, in a communication sent to Colonel Canby to inform him that Colorado's First regiment was coming to his assistance, said:

"You will find this regiment, I hope, a most efficient one and of great support to you. It has had, of course, no experience in the

Lieutenant-Colonel Samuel F. Tappan, of the First Colorado Regiment.
(From a war-time photograph in the State Historical and Natural History Society's collection.)

field, but I trust that their enthusiasm and patriotic bravery will make amends, and more than that, for their lack of active service in the past."

In Civil War times soldiers were not moved from one station to another in sleeping cars, as nowadays, and there were no railroads west of the Missouri river. Until these Colorado troops reached the

Santa Fé trail they marched through a section of country in which there was scarcely anything worthy the name of a broken wagon road. When the companies from Camp Weld had arrived at Pueblo, and those from Fort Wise at old Fort Bent, both on the Arkansas river, they learned for the first time, through advices from Colonel Canby, that his Fort Craig forces had been vanquished at Valverdé and nearly all of his field guns captured, and that the Confederates were moving in triumph northward along the Rio Grandé. They were urged to hasten to his relief. Discarding everything except actual necessities, the two divisions immediately struck out southward, advancing as rapidly as they were able through the several inches of snow that covered the country, and making about forty miles a day. The columns were united on the headwaters of the Purgatoire river, at Gray's ranch, near the present city of Trinidad. On the way the men were deeply impressed by the grandeur of the winter scenery around the majestic Spanish peaks to their right. They followed the Santa Fé trail through the wild, picturesque gorge between Simpson's rest and Fisher's peak, and on over the Raton mountains. As they reached the summit of the last height several eagles came sailing in a circle above them. A private in Company D called out: "Let's shoot them." But Captain Downing prevented this by shouting: "These are the birds of Liberty; and they betoken victory to us!" Then the whole company gave three cheers for the eagles.

As the regiment was preparing to bivouac at the close of the day, March 8th, on the southern slope of the Raton mountains, and expecting to have a greatly needed rest for the night after the toilsome climbing of the opposite slope, there dashed into the camp a courier from Colonel Gabriel R. Paul, of the Fourth regiment New Mexico Volunteers, and commander at Fort Union, with the startling information that General Sibley was already in possession of Albuquerqué and Santa Fé, was fast enlisting volunteers there, and completing his arrangements to march upon and attack the fort, in which were only some 400 regulars, and about the same number of volunteers, to defend it. On a stirring appeal to the regiment to render speedy aid to its garrison, all of the men expressed their willingness to set out again without delay, carrying "only their arms and blankets." Through the darkness up to day-light, and over a route to which they were not accustomed, they marched thirty miles to Maxwell's ranch on the Cimarron river, making in all sixty-seven they had traveled continuously since the morning before, and ninety-two in the previous thirty-six hours. Here they were compelled to halt from "sheer exhaustion." Some of their

Fort Union.
(From a wood engraving in "El Gringo," by W. W. H. Davis, 1857.)

animals, "on account of overwork and underfeed," had dropped dead in the harness on the road. One or two companies had been mounted for the movement to Fort Union, for scouting purposes, but the others covered these extraordinary distances on foot—a proof of the men's great physical endurance. After a brief rest, the Colorado volunteers proceeded toward the threatened post, encountering on the first day a bitterly cold and furious windstorm, a mountain hurricane, which showered and blinded them with driven snow, dust and sand. But in the evening of the second day, March 10th, they were joyously welcomed by the officers and soldiers at Fort Union, and also by the governor of New Mexico, who, with the other territorial officers, had abandoned Santa Fé and made Las Végas, thirty miles south of the fort, the emergency seat of their government. The governor, in a communication to the secretary of state, at Washington, written at Fort Union the next day, said, evidently in contrast to many of the volunteers of his own territory, that the Colorado troops were "men that from all accounts can be relied upon," and added that his "militia have all dispersed, and have gone to preparing their lands for the coming harvest, and this is by far the best use that could be made of them." The territory was panic-stricken. Colonel Canby, who had not learned of the arrival of the "Pike's Peakers," as the Confederates afterward called them, in advices to Colonel Paul, at Fort Union, dated March 16th, instructed the latter to hold that post at all hazards, but to order Fort Garland, in Colorado, to be entirely destroyed if the enemy menaced it by moving on northward.

Within three weeks after the Colorado regiment had marched into Fort Union the sanguine invaders of New Mexico were hurriedly preparing to get out of the country "as quick as the Lord will let us."

The regiment remained at Fort Union until the 22d of March, undergoing in the meantime almost daily drilling. Here, also, the men were completely supplied and equipped with regulation clothing, arms and ammunition from the government stores. Colonel Slough assumed command of all of the troops at the post, by reason of the seniority of his commission. Between him and Colonel Paul arose a difference of opinion in respect to the execution of the orders of Colonel Canby. The latter held that only by staying at the fort until otherwise directed could the former assist in accomplishing the ends desired to be attained. The former maintained that, on the contrary, he was empowered by these orders "to be governed" by his "own judgment and discretion;" that he was instructed, "if joined by a sufficient force," to act independently against the enemy; and that by advancing over the same route which they must pursue in reaching the fort, he could defend it as well as by staying, and could better "harass the enemy," "obstruct their movements and cut off their supplies," as required, and,

Present Condition of Kozlowski's Ranch.

(From one of the author's photographs.)

at the same time, better discover an opportunity for "protecting Santa Fé from depredation." The sequel proved, as will be seen, that his decision was veritably and immeasurably wise. Beside this, his Colorado soldiers were endowed with such rugged energy that they could not longer endure the routine of petty duties and the severity of discipline incident to garrison life. Against the vigor-

Kozlowski's Spring in the Bank of the Creek Back of His Ranch.
(From one of the author's photographs.)

ous protest of Colonel Paul, Colonel Slough announced that, in his departure from the post, he could "not consent to leave any portion of his command behind." Accordingly, on the date above given, he began his march toward Santa Fé by the way of Las Végas. He had, when he left Fort Union, beside his own First Colorado regiment, Captain Ford's company of unattached Colorado volunteers, and one of the Fourth regiment of New Mexico volunteers, and of regulars a battalion of infantry, three detachments of cavalry and two light batteries of four guns each—making in all 1,342 men. A small number of other regulars and volunteers, con-

6

sidered sufficient to guard the property in the fort, was assigned to the charge of its former commander.

On the 25th of March, in the afternoon, Major Chivington, with nearly a third of the advancing column, started from Bernal Springs, aiming to reach Santa Fé as soon as possible, and to surprise and expel the enemy, reported then to be only "about one hundred men, with two pieces of artillery." Chivington's force consisted of sixty men of Company A, Captain Wynkoop; sixty of Company D, Captain Downing; sixty of Company E, Captain Anthony, and eighty-eight mounted men of Company F, under Captain Cook and Lieutenants Nelson and Marshall, all of the First Colorado. Twenty eight of Company C, six of Company D, six of —, and ten of K, Third Regular Cavalry, under Captain Howland and Lieutenants Wall and Falvey; fifty of Company E, Third Regular Cavalry, commanded by Captain Walker and Lieutenant Banks; fifty of Companies D and G, First Regular Cavalry, under Captain Lord and Lieutenant Bernard. In all, 418 enlisted men. Late in the night these troops stopped and encamped at Kozlowski's ranch, a short distance south of the ruined Pécos mission. Here they were told that some Confederate scouts, heavily armed and splendidly mounted, were in the neighborhood, and had visited the place early in the evening. Before they left in the direction of La Gloriéta pass they had inquired: "Have any Yanks been seen about here?" Of course, they were answered in the negative, as none had then made an appearance. At once was introduced a new policy into the Federal conduct of the war in the territory—one that was bold, vigorous and aggressive in the treatment of the Texans. Lieutenant Nelson, of Captain Cook's company, was sent with twenty men to find and capture these scouting Confederates, which he effected before daybreak at Pigeon's ranch, just within the eastern entrance to this pass, without firing a shot, and then immediately returned with the prisoners to camp. Among these were two officers, one, Lieutenant McIntyre, who had formerly belonged to Colonel Canby's staff, and had served with him at the battle of Valverdé, but had deserted to the enemy, and the other, Captain Hall, had been a well-known resident of Denver City. At this time Major

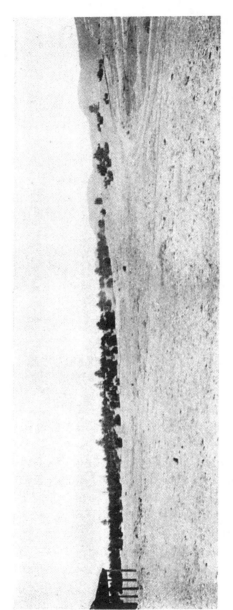

Site of Camp Lewis, the Encampment of the Colorado Volunteers at Kozlowski's Ranch in March, 1862.

(From one of the author's photographs.)

Chivington learned that the advance of General Sibley's army was at the farther end of La Gloriéta pass, and was expected to move the following day toward Fort Union.

Kozlowski's ranch, at which Chivington's detachment encamped, became closely associated with the operations of Colonel Slough's command while in this region. The adobe building in the accompanying view is the largest of several in the group, and stands on the right bank of a stream that empties into the Pécos river. Beyond it, in the somewhat deep channel, is a grove of cottonwood trees, and under them a copious spring of pure water flows from crevices in the sandstone rock. This furnished a reason for the location of the ranch at the place. Here for many years were provided excellent accommodations for the stages, freighters and other conveyances traveling on the Santa Fé trail, which crossed the stream at this point. In the picture, in front of the building, stands, in military attitude, Martin Kozlowski, the owner. He was born April 24, 1827, in the city of Warsaw, Poland; took part in the revolution of his countrymen in 1848 against Germany; was a refugee for two years in England, where he married; came to America and enlisted in 1853 in the First Dragoons of the regular army of the United States; served five years in New Mexico, fighting the Indians, and was mustered out in 1858, when he settled down here on his 600 acres of land. He complimented the Union troops thus: "When they camped on my place, and while they made my tavern their hospital for over two months after their battles in the cañon, they never robbed me of anything, not even a chicken."

As long as these Federal troops were here, they made their camp on the bluff covered with cedar bushes, as appears in the view. The camp was named after Captain William H. Lewis, from Fort Dodge, Kansas, a brave and efficient officer of the Fifth Infantry of the regular army. At the left of the view is seen a section of the front portico to Kozlowski's main structure, and at the right the Santa Fé trail winds down the northern slope of the bluff toward the ford in the stream. In the distance are some of the nearer heights of the Pécos mésa, just in front of which now runs the Santa Fé Railway, that enters La Gloriéta pass five miles back.

THE FIGHT IN THE APACHE CAÑON.

At eight o'clock in the morning of March 26th the detachment of troops under Major Chivington broke camp at Kozlowski's ranch, to make a reconnoissance in force, without artillery, toward the capital of the territory. In passing the ruins of the Pécos pueblo and of the old Franciscan mission they closely observed the extensive remains of these structures, which to them were both novel and impressive. They arrived in due time at Pigeon's ranch, which holds a very prominent place in the history of the campaign.

This, also, was a hostelry, the largest and most convenient on the trail from Las Végas to Santa Fé. Though at the time of this writing it is greatly dilapidated, it is still the dwelling of a family. It was so called after the nickname applied before the Civil War to its proprietor, Alexander Vallé, a Franco-American, from his peculiar style of dancing at parties. He was genial, vivacious and obliging, a popular host with travelers for years, and became such to the Union soldiers entertained by him. His ranch was located in a defile of the cañon, so narrow that it was fully occupied by the buildings, the road, and an arroyo, in which flows a small stream some months in a year. In the accompanying view is seen the principal structure, the rear of which formed a kind of Asiatic caravansary, where guests could lodge by themselves and eat their own meals. Beyond was a double corral for enclosing and protecting loaded wagons, and to it was attached sheds with stalls for draft horses and mules. Back of these, running up well into a ravine, was a strong adobe wall that surrounded a yard in which teams could also be kept and fed. The square indentation in the upper part of the nearest end of the building, partially roofed, is said to have been made by a cannon ball fired in the engagement that occurred at this ranch on the second day after Major Chivington's force stopped here.

But this detachment, after proceeding fully a mile and a half up the pass, gained the summit of its divide about two o'clock in

Present Condition of Pigeon's Ranch.
(From one of the author's photographs.)

the afternoon, and the advance guard, in descending the opposite slope and through a narrow gulch, came, at a short turn in the road and in the midst of a thicket of trees and bushes, unexpectedly upon a scouting party, from a larger force a mile or so back, of thirty mounted Texans led by a lieutenant, none of whom had any knowledge of the approach of these Federal troops from Fort Union. They were taken prisoners without any casualties to either side. One of the captors rushed back to the main body under Major Chivington, shouting, "We've got them corraled this time!" and exploding an imperative to the "boys," as he designated them, in language too vigorous to be repeated here. The forward movement was continued by the whole column hurriedly, but cautiously, for three-fourths of a mile down to a point where the trail bends to the right and enters a long open space in the Apache cañon proper, the western section of La Gloriéta pass. Our illustration of this locality ("the Upper Battlefield in the Apache Cañon") is from a photograph taken from the track of the Santa Fé Railway, which runs well up on the side of the cañon, that here turns abruptly to the southwest. Gloriéta mountain is seen in the distance. A deep arroyo winds down through the depression immediately in front, and just beyond it the old Santa Fé trail passes. The main body of the Confederates entered this field on the left, low down in the view, and their scouting party had been captured on the right among the trees at the extreme upper end. The Union column rushed down into the field from that direction, and sought shelter at first from the cannon shots of the invaders behind and to the east of the ridge that nearly crosses, transversely, the upper part of the cañon.

This vanguard of Sibley's brigade, under the command of Major Pyron, having marched about two hours from their camp at the western end of La Gloriéta pass, arrived on the nearest portion of the field seen in this view, with entire confidence that they would be successful in their expedition to Fort Union. How extreme must have been their surprise when they here discovered, without any forwarning, the presence of a determined foe, only a third of a mile away from them, eager for an encounter. Then were exhibited the superb push, daring and hardiness of the frontiersmen who

constituted the bulk of both commands. On this spot began the
armed conflict—brief, fearless and decisive—between these detachments, in one of which were "Baylor's Babes," as they were familiarly called, and in the other the "Pet Lambs of Colorado." The
issue at stake was the immediate mastery and the future civil control of an immense region in the West and Southwest.

View of the Upper Battlefield in the Apache Canon, Looking North.
(From one of the author's photographs.)

The Confederate force halted at once on seeing the Federal; un-
furled in defiance its red flag, on which was displayed the emblem
of Texas, the "Lone Star," and planted in the road its artillery,
two fine howitzers, guarded by mounted infantry. Shells and grape
shot were quickly thrown at close quarters in the direction of the
Union troops, who crowded in some confusion of formation to the
left into shelter from the fire. By vigorous measures Major Chivington at once restored order among his men. Those mounted were
sent to the rear in charge of Captain George W. Howland, of the
Third United States Cavalry, with instructions to hurl themselves
upon the Texan artillerymen in case they saw these in retreat; and

Captain Cook, with his mounted company of the First Colorado Volunteers, was instructed to join Howland in this movement. Captains Wynkoop and Anthony, with their companies, were deployed at double-quick as skirmishers on the mountainside among the thick evergreen trees to the left of the field. These two were soon joined by Captain Charles J. Walker with a company of regular cavalry dismounted. Captain Downing with his company of the First Colorado, as skirmishers, hastened along the irregular mountainside to the right. Smaller parties of other volunteers and regulars were stationed in front, doubtless under the protection afforded by the low transverse ridge of ground lying in the back part of the field.

The rapid firing of the skirmishers upon the flanks of the Texans made "their position in the road untenable," and they retired speedily with their guns to the lower end of the open space, where the cañon turns abruptly to the right, and disappeared down it about three-fourths of a mile to a place where the mountain ranges draw closer to each other and affording far better advantages for defense. Captain Howland failed to lead his command, as ordered, against the foe leaving the field in a broken condition. The Federals collected their scattered forces, and followed with caution to a point where there is a sharp projection of rock into the cañon, and here they halted under this cover to complete plans for another attack. On the way they had been saluted with an occasional cannon ball from the road, and with buck shot and rifle bullets from rocks on both sides of it, by the retreating Confederates.

The Texans as repulsed withdrew from the upper battlefield on the Santa Fé trail, which is seen in the illustration of that field, as well as in the picture of the lower one; crossed a bridge of logs, of which the one in the foreground of the latter view is a successor, and then removed it so as to cut off an immediate pursuit by the Union cavalry; posted their howitzers in the defile just beyond the bridge, where they could command the road, and completely covered the mountain slopes on both sides with their supports of the artillery. The same arroyo runs through both battlefields, generally from twenty to twenty-five feet deep, and with perpendicular banks.

The bridge by which it was spanned was at least sixteen feet long, and furnished the only convenient crossing from one side to the other. So any front attack by either cavalry or infantry must be made along a very narrow margin, and the destruction of the bridge, it was expected, would stop any further advance of the Northern troops in that direction. Beside, this structure was located beneath a high ridge, over the top of which, as from behind a bastion wall of a fort, shots in volleys could be discharged in the very faces of an attacking army and with comparative safety to the defenders. The distribution of the skirmishers in supporting the battery, especially those of an entire company on this high ridge, would frustrate, in all probability, an attempt successfully to flank the position. Indeed, it was a formidable one, and could be taken by a small force only by the exhibition of surpassing bravery and skillful maneuver.

Within an eighth of a mile of the place, and with the utmost promptness, Major Chivington proceeded to execute plan adopted for the assault upon this natural fortress. He dismounted the regular cavalry under Captain Howland, and united the men with the infantry commanded by the intrepid Captain Downing, who was directed to climb the steep and rough mountainside on the right above the Texan skirmishers, and by the close and incessant firing of his men drive the Confederates out of the bottom of the cañon. Captains Wynkoop and Anthony, with their companies, were ordered to outflank the skirmishers on the left in the same manner, to assist in effecting this result. Captain Cook's mounted company was placed in reserve out of the range of the howitzers, and told to charge, at a given signal, upon the Confederates when they showed any disposition to abandon the field. The rest of the Federal forces were required to make a movement directly in front. Among these was Major Chivington on horseback, "with a pistol in each hand and one or two under his arms," giving special orders for the charge "with great energy." "Of commanding presence, and dressed in full regimentals, he was a conspicuous mark for the Texan sharpshooters." One of their officers, taken prisoner, averred that he emptied his revolver three times at the major, and made his company fire a volley at him. But he galloped on unhurt through the storm of bullets. Vallé, of Pigeon's ranch, said of him, in this fight: "'E poot 'iz 'ead down and foight loike a mahd bull." The companies on the flanks performed their difficult task with great celerity. In an hour's time the supports of the Confederate battery were driven from the mountainsides to the center of the battlefield, still fighting "like tigers at bay." At the opportune moment, Captain Cook's men tore down the road in a body, and with a hair-

Near View of the Strategic Bridge in the Lower Battlefield in the Apache Canon.
(From one of the author's photographs.)

raising yell compelled all of their 103 horses but one, which fell back upon its rider into the arroyo and injured him for life, to leap across the chasm at the bridge. Then they immediately, in the midst of the missiles that rained upon them from the high ridges, charged three times forward and back through the fleeing and crowded ranks of the Texans, running over them, trampling them down, and scattering them in every direction—"as gallant an onset in war as ever was made." Their guns "proved too light-footed" to be overtaken. By the time the Confederates were, in terror and disorder, rushing along the cañon at and beyond the bold curve in it to the left through the gorge seen in the farther part of the view,

Captain Downing and his men had raced across the mountain to the right, and were pouring into them a "most galling and destructive fire," which drove them into the base of the mountain on the opposite side of the cañon, where his company, with those of Captains Wynkoop and Anthony, took about fifty of them prisoners.

Captain Samuel H. Cook.
(From a war-time photograph in the State Historical and Natural History Society's collection.)

Evening coming on, further pursuit was abandoned.

While the number of men on each side was comparatively small, and the engagement occupied but two or three hours, the fight was furious while it lasted. The Texans were badly used up, and, beside their heavy losses in killed and wounded, some seventy or eighty of them were prisoners. Seven of their commanding officers were among the slain. Only one Union officer, Captain Cook, of Company F, First Colorado, was hit in the fray. He was struck in the thigh by an ounce ball and three buck shot, and a minute or two later in the foot by a bullet. But to hearten his men he made light of his agonizing wounds. By a distressing accident, Lieutenant Marshall, of Cook's company, lost his life, being killed by the discharge of a prisoner's musket, which he held at its muzzle end in striking it across a rock to break it.

It should be noted by the reader that none of the Colorado volunteers had ever before engaged in a battle. Among these a private captured a Texas captain hidden in the arroyo, and, having disarmed him, led him to the rear. In a house, still standing in the lower battlefield, fifteen Confederates were made prisoners, when they might easily have defended themselves in it for a longer time. After one of the Texans had surrendered he concealed himself behind a rock and deliberately shot at Captain Logan, who seized a rifle and mortally wounded him on the spot. The defeated Confederates returned to the camp they had left in the morning, sent a flag of truce late in the evening, and requested the privilege of burying their dead and caring for their wounded. At the lower end of the upper battlefield some skeletons of these devoted victims of war recently have been washed by the rains from a bank of the arroyo. On this field grape shot are still plowed up in the spring of the year. Major Chivington's troops left the scene of this engagement early that night, as they feared the return of Major Pyron's command, largely reenforced by a detachment from the reserves in the camp at Galistéo, and they hastily gathered up their dead and wounded, and several of the wounded Confederates, and carried them to Pigeon's ranch, where a hospital was established, and then they encamped here for the remainder of the night. Still, a small force of cavalry was held in the Apache cañon as a rear guard until later in the night.

The following are extracts from a letter written April 30, 1862, at Socorro, New Mexico, by a paroled Texan prisoner, to his wife, and placed in the hands of a comrade to be given by him to her. It was found, with a large number of others, at Mésilla, after the last of these prisoners had left the territory by the succeedingly July. It strengthens some of the statements made in the foregoing description of the fighting in the Apache cañon, and adds several new items of interest:

"We felt like heroes, having had a fight at Fort Craig, scaring the Mexicans to flight, and driving the regular soldiers into the fort, and getting past with our whole army, and cutting off all supplies and relief to the fort. We marched up the country with the fixed determination to wrench this country from the United States government, and we all thought it would soon be in our hands. But what a mistake! Having marched up beyond Santa Fé we were again met by the enemy, from Fort Union, and, after three battles with them, all of us who were not killed or taken prisoners were obliged to destroy everything they had and flee to the mountains for their lives, and to get out of the country, the Lord only knows how. We are among those taken prisoners. * * *.

"Our company, with the Second and Third regiments, reached Santa Fé the 16th or 17th of March. In two days our regiment came up. We were to wait a short time, and then march on and take Fort Union, which, we thought, was ours already; and then New Mexico would belong to the new government of the South, and it would then be so easy to cut off all communication from California. On the 22d six hundred of us were ordered to march to Apache cañon to stand picket. Here we all dismounted, and our horses were sent to a ranch, on account of being worn out by hard riding. One company went with the horses to guard them, and we went into camp at the mouth of the cañon. On the 26th we got word that the enemy was coming down the cañon in the shape of 200 Mexicans and about 200 regulars. Out we marched with the two cannons, expecting an easy victory; but what a mistake! Instead of Mexicans and regulars, they were *regular demons,* upon whom iron and lead had no effect, in the shape of Pike's Peakers, from the Denver City gold mines, where we thought of going about a year ago.

"As I said, up the cañon we went for about four miles, where we met the enemy coming at double-quick, but our grape and shell soon stopped them; but before we could form in line of battle their infantry were upon the hills on both sides of us, shooting us down like sheep. The order was given to retreat down the cañon, which we did about a mile. The cannons and a company of men stopped to check the enemy, while the rest of us went down the cañon a mile farther, to where the road makes a short bend to the left, with high and ragged mountains on both sides. In these mountains were stationed about one hundred and fifty men; forty more were stationed in and about some houses on the right of the road, I among the number. This was no sooner done than up came the cannons, with the enemy at their heels; but when they saw us ready to receive them they stopped, but only for a short time, for in a few minutes they could be seen on the mountains jumping from rock to rock like so many mountain sheep. They had no sooner got within shooting distance of us than up came a company of cavalry at full charge, with swords and revolvers drawn, looking like so many flying devils. On they came to what I supposed was destruction; but nothing like lead or iron seemed to stop them, for we were pouring it into them from every side like hail in a storm. In a moment these devils had run the gauntlet for half a mile, and were fighting hand to hand with our men in the road. The houses that I spoke of before were seven or eight hundred yards to the right of the road, with a wide ditch [arroyo] between it and them. Here we

View of the Lower Battlefield in the Apache Canon. The Fighting Took Place on the Hills and in the Valley Beyond the Bridge.
(From one of the author's photographs.)

felt safe, but again we were mistaken, for no sooner did they see us than some of them turned their horses, jumped the ditch and like demons came charging on us. It looked as if their horses' feet never touched the ground, until they were among us.

"It was a grand sight. We shot as fast as we could, and as that handful of men jumped the ditch and charged on us we expected to shoot the last one before they reached us. But luck was against us, and after fighting hand to hand with them, and our comrades being shot and cut down every moment, we were obliged to surrender. Now, who do you suppose it was that came charging and nearly running over me, with a revolver pointing at my head, ordering me to lay down my arms and consider myself a prisoner? This I did, for I knew that the next moment would be my last if I did not. It was George Lowe, brother-in-law of Mr. Whitney, that keeps the store at Portage, Wis. You know him well. I knew him as soon as I saw him, but he did not recognize me, and I was very glad of it. * * *

"How any one of these men who charged us escaped death will ever be a wonder to me. Our men who were fighting them in the road were soon obliged to retreat, and the fight was over. About eighty of us who were taken prisoners were soon marched off to Fort Union. How many were killed and wounded I don't know, but there must have been a large number. Such a sight I never want to see again. As I was marched off the field I saw some men with their heads nearly shot off, some with their arms or legs shot off, and one poor man, that belonged to my company, I saw lying against a tree with his brains all shot out. Henry Asher had an arm shot off, but made out to escape. He was standing by my side when he was shot. The men that charged us seemed to have charmed lives, for if they had not they could never have reached us alive."

In the morning of the 27th of March Major Chivington's men were engaged at Pigeon's ranch in burying their dead in an open field a quarter of a mile down the cañon, in attending to the needs of the wounded they had brought here the evening before, and in arranging to send their prisoners on to Fort Union. They had been joined during the night by a reinforcement of 300 infantry and cavalry from Bernal Springs, where Colonel Slough had his reserves in camp, for the purpose of aiding to resist any farther advance, if it should be attempted, of the Texans at the western extremity of the pass, which locality was then known as Johnson's ranch, and is now called Cañoncito. Fortunately, a quantity of flour and corn, stored by the invaders a few days before in a building near Pigeon's ranch, was found and confiscated by these hungry men, who converted it into their morning rations. The water taken from a well here, then the only supply, proved to be insufficient for them and their horses, and so they returned in a body to their camp at Kozlowski's, where, as we have already seen, there was a copious spring. Here, or more probably on the ridge just south of the ruined old Pécos mission, the entire force, the remaining detachment at Bernal Springs having arrived, were reunited in the afternoon and night following, and the plans formed for the movements on the next day.

THE DECISIVE BATTLE.

At the opening of the battle in Apache cañon, in the afternoon of March 26th, Major Pyron, in charge of the Confederate force engaged there, sent a swift courier to Lieutenant-Colonel Scurry, the Confederate commander at Galistéo, about fifteen miles distant, to inform the latter that he "was engaged in a sharp conflict" with the enemy, and to urge that a force be "hastened to his relief." Colonel Scurry, in his report of the battle of La Gloriéta, says that "the critical condition of Major Pyron and his gallant comrades was made known to the command, and in ten minutes the column was formed and the order to march given."

By daylight next morning not only this detachment, but all of the Confederate reserves at Galistéo, and their entire baggage train, had reached, "in a cold night march," Pyron's encampment at Johnson's ranch, at the western end of La Gloriéta pass. An agreement had been made between Chivington and Pyron to suspend hostilities until eight o'clock the next morning, and after that hour an attack some time during the day was expected by Colonel Scurry. He, therefore, early examined the location and its surroundings very thoroughly, and satisfied himself that it afforded an exceedingly strong position for defense. He then stationed his troops so as to command every approach to it. The attack not occurring, he decided to move forward soon after sunrise the next day, March 28th, through the pass, with all portions of which he was well acquainted; to leave his train behind with only "a small wagon guard," so that his progress might not be impeded, and to gain the level ground near the ruins of the Pécos pueblo, where he would offer battle to the Federal troops, anticipating a decisive victory similar to that won at Valverdé.

Accordingly, on that day, it being next to the last in the week, he began, at the appointed hour, his march with three Texan regiments having seventeen partially filled companies, with an independent one of volunteers called *Brigandes*, and with an efficient

(98)

battery of three guns, a total of about 1,100 men. His soldiers had enjoyed a season of rest, though somewhat brief to about a fourth of them, and nearly all of them already had been under fire. There prevailed among them the fullest confidence in the ability of their leader, and complete harmony in their ranks. The field officers had shown themselves to be cool, fearless and aggressive in battle, with the skill of veterans in handling small bodies of troops. The whole command was animated with the expectation of soon reaching Fort Union and capturing it with all of its vast army supplies. Then the region from the lower ranges of the Rocky mountains west to the Colorado river would be practically in their possession.

Instead of on an open space of ground near the Pécos pueblo, it was on the eastern decline of La Gloriéta pass, among thick pine trees and cedar bushes, within a mile to the west of Pigeon's ranch, that Colonel Scurry first halted his forces about half-past eight o'clock in the morning, as he had then discovered a considerable body of Federal soldiers occupying the last-named place. This was a far more advantageous position for both an attack and a defense, where two small armies were about to fight each other, though undoubtedly favoring the former movement rather than the latter. Here had been formed by a local glacier from Gloriéta mountain a series of terminal moraines, two of which are low bluffs, merging on the south into bold, rocky elevations, and lying nearly parallel to each other, and not far apart. The northern ends of these evidently had been broken through or washed away by a large, rapid stream caused by the melting of the immense deposit of ice in the pass and on the mountainsides, and leaving a narrow and deeper depression along them, through which now run the old Santa Fé trail and the Gloriéta arroyo. These features of the place, together with the abrupt slopes of the cañon and the high ledges of rock in the rear and in the front of Pigeon's ranch, served to determine largely the positions taken, the maneuvers adopted, and the results attained in the fierce and prolonged struggle had here on that day.

Soon after the Texans began their advance in the morning from Johnson's ranch, the Federal troops in camp at Kozlowski's started in two columns to reconnoiter in force the former, with the view

View of the Western Entrance to La Glorieta Pass, at Johnson's Ranch, or Canoncito.

(From one of the author's photographs.)

of ascertaining the Confederates' position and actual strength, and of harassing them as much as possible, if the opportunity should be offered. About one-third of the command was ordered, under the charge of Major Chivington, to "push forward" to the western end of the pass by a circuitous route over the mountains to the south of it, and at that end to occupy the heights on the same side of the Apache cañon, and to observe thoroughly the condition of the enemy's encampment beneath. Nearly all of the remainder of the command, namely, Companies C, D, F, G, I and K (some of which had been reduced by detachments for guard and other special duties), a broken company of New Mexican volunteers, two small detachments of regular cavalry, and two light batteries of regular artillery, the latter being directed by Captain John F. Ritter and Lieutenant Ira W. Claflin, in all not more than 700 men, were marched by Colonel Slough to Pigeon's ranch, with the purpose of traversing the pass throughout, if he should find that the invaders had retired toward Santa Fé. The Confederate commander during that day supposed that Slough's entire force, about equal in number to his own, was in front of him, as he had no knowledge of Major Chivington's expedition, which had left Slough with scarcely more than half that number. Furthermore, only slightly over a third of Slough's officers and men had ever been under fire. A portion of them, including the batteries, had reached the camp very late in the preceding night, having traveled thirty-five miles in the previous sixteen hours, and, consequently, were greatly fatigued, and thus ill prepared to endure the intense excitement and supreme exertions that attended the desperate conflict of La Gloriéta.

Beside these conditions the men entertained no cordial and trustful feelings toward their colonel, which was due to his habitual austerity and his lack of military experience. In fact, some of them, beyond doubt unjustly, suspected his loyalty to the cause of the Union, on account of his former political affiliations. One of his captains declared, years afterward: "I watched him closely during the fight at Pigeon's ranch, and if I had discovered any movement or order of his intended to be favorable at the time to the enemy, I would have shot him on the spot." Ovando J. Hollister, an intelligent and observant private soldier in the First Colorado, who kept a diary while in the service, and in 1863 published a pamphlet, based on his daily notes, containing much of the history of the regiment up to that year, referring to an incident which occurred at the time the two divisions of the regiment were joined on the Purgatoire river, on the march to Fort Union, says in his publication:

"Our camp this evening on the Purgatoire, March 7th, augmented by seven hundred men, has the bustle and hum of a small town. We 'fell in' and gave the colonel three cheers and a tiger. He raised his cap, but did not speak. How little some men understand human nature. He had been our colonel six months, had never spoken to us, and on the eve of an important expedition, after a long absence, could not see that a few words were indispensable to a good understanding. He has a noble appearance, but the men seem to lack confidence in him. Why, I can not tell—nor can they, I think. His aristocratic style savors more of eastern society than of the free-and-easy border, to which he should have become acclimated, but that it is bred in the bone."

The different parts of Slough's column, with the cavalry in advance, and the supply train of at least one hundred wagons with their guards in the rear, arrived at this ranch and its immediate vicinity between half-past eight and ten o'clock in the forenoon. Some of them were halted here for an hour and a half for rest, and others for a briefer period before the time last mentioned. No apprehension was felt that the foe they wished to encounter was already within a short distance of them. All of the companies of infantry broke ranks and stacked their arms, to visit the wounded left here since the fight in the Apache cañon, and to fill their canteens from Pigeon's well, as a supply of water could not be obtained again until they had reached the western end of the pass. The cavalry was sent forward in the charge of Captain Gurden Chapin, of the Seventh United States Infantry, the assistant adjutant-general under Colonel Slough, with some pickets ahead, to reconnoiter. Very soon the latter rushed back with the information that the Texans in force were in a position to attack, about 800 yards in front, and hidden in a thick grove. At once the bugles sounded the assembly, men seized their arms, companies formed in rank, preliminary orders were issued, but before arrangements to resist the expected onset of the enemy could be completed, grape shot and shell from their guns were crashing through the tops of the cottonwood trees at the ranch over the heads of the Federal troops.

The battle opened in a gulch, about half a mile west of Pigeon's ranch, and lying between two moraines, which extend from the road toward the range of mountains on the south side of the pass. The one on the left slopes down northward to the road from a considerable elevation, and that on the right has a comparatively level top and runs back several hundred yards. On this level Lieutenant-Colonel Scurry formed his first line of battle, stretching across the cañon from near an arroyo some rods north of the road "up into the pine forest" to the south. Just before reaching it he dismounted his cavalry, and sent the men into action on foot. His artillery, which was commanded by Lieutenant James Bradford, who had distinguished himself in the battle of Valverdé, was ordered to the front on the brow of this ridge, and to begin firing immediately upon the Federals, who were advancing rapidly toward the opposite ridge. The cavalry sent forward by Colonel Slough to reconnoiter had already entered this gulch, and on discovering the position of the Texan guns the force was directed by Captain Charles J. Walker, in charge of one of the companies, to move at once "into the timber" on their left, to dismount, and to commence "skirmishing on foot." They were soon relieved by the arrival of other troops and the batteries from the ranch, and were stationed on the high ridge to the north and beyond Pigeon's house. In the meantime Colonel Scurry had arranged his infantry into three columns, deploying that on his right toward the southern end of the ridge he was occupying, and placing it under the command of Major Pyron, who had opened for the Confederate side the encounter at Valverdé. Another was held at the middle near the artillery, under the charge of Major Raguet, while the third was led by himself to the northern end of the ridge and across the old Santa Fé trail.

The illustrations of the field of the second fight in La Gloriéta pass, on pages 104 and 105, are halves of one photographic view, and represent the landscape at the eastern entrance to the pass.

View of a Part of the Field of the Second Battle in La Glorieta Pass.

(From one of the author's photographs.)

The picture on the opposite page is a continuation, to the right, of this view.

View of a Part of the Field of the Second Battle in La Gloriota Pass.

(From one of the author's photographs.)

This is a continuation, to the right, of the view on the opposite page.

Pigeon's famous adobe hostelry and its outbuildings appear in the left of the view on page 105, and occupy the point from which all of the movements of the Federal forces radiated in the Gloriéta engagements. The Santa Fé Railway, which is hidden in the view, and the Santa Fé trail, enter the pass here, the course of the latter past Pigeon's ranch being visible. The height in the middle distance is a part of the Pécos mésa.

To Lieutenant-Colonel Tappan was assigned early in the day the immediate command of the Colorado volunteers and the regular artillery present under Colonel Slough. As soon as his men had recovered from their surprise at the approach and sudden attack of the Texan troops, the following disposition of them was at once made by their leader: Captain Ritter's battery of four guns, supported by Captain Sopris' company of infantry, was sent at double-quick to take position on the road on the north of the open space in the battlefield at the lower end of the eastern moraine; and Lieutenant Claflin's battery, also of four guns, supported by Captain Robbins' company, to be stationed farther up on this moraine to the south and among the trees in sight of the enemy, who was across the gulch on its west side. Captain Downing's company was deployed farther to the south, and Captain Mailie's company of Germans, in charge of Lieutenant Charles Kerber, to the north, in the cañon arroyo and on the slope beyond, both to skirmish from elevations on the flanks of the Texans, finding shelter among the thick trees. The other companies of infantry, with the cavalry, were retired down the pass, to be held as reserves and to protect the supply train in their rear.

At once the fighting along both lines became general and furious. The discharges of the artillery seemed incessant, and the roar of them sounded at a distance in all directions like a heavy and continuous drumming of a military band. Many of the shots were imbedded in the trees between and around the opposing batteries, and the indentations or scars made by them remain to this day on scores of the pine and cedar trunks still standing. Occasionally one of these was thus marred on both sides, being hit by guns fired from both ridges. Grape shot, pieces of exploded shells and rarely a cannon ball may yet be dug from the ground where the batteries stood, and in the immediate vicinity. The commander of the Texan artillery was soon severely wounded and borne from the field, his horses killed, and his men retreating in disorder. Upon them and the supporting infantry the minie balls from the Springfield rifles in the unerring hands of the Colorado skirmishers told with deadly effect. Suddenly Colonel Scurry discovered the company under Lieutenant Kerber approaching and passing his left flank under the cover of an irrigating ditch about 200 yards away. He dashed with his column across a clearing in an enclosed field and into the midst of these determined Germans, and with pistol and *machete* in hand struggled desperately face to face with them, who used their bayonets vigorously, but who were forced to fall back among the bushes, trees and rocks on the abrupt slope in the northern end of the main battlefield, leaving behind many of their number killed or wounded. One of the dead was the courageous Lieutenant John Baker, whose fearfully mutilated body was found by the burial party next morning stripped of his clothing. Of him and the manner of his death Lieutenant-Colonel Tappan said in his report:

"Lieutenant Baker was severely wounded during the early part of the engagement, and afterward beaten to death by the enemy with the butt of a musket or club, and his body stripped of its clothing. He was found the next morning, his head scarcely recognizable, so horribly mangled. He fought gallantly, and the vengeance of the foe pursued him after death."

But it was thought by some of his comrades that this awful work was due to vagabond Mexicans who had followed the Confederate forces.

Lieutenant Baker had led the forward division of his company along the ditch above mentioned, to a point almost opposite the Texan artillery on higher ground to his left, and then, drawing his sword and waving it, he called to his men: "Let's capture the guns!" At that instant he was struck down. Both he and Kerber had served in the regular army of the United States, and with their prompt military skill had brought their company first on the battlefield.

On the opposite flank of the Confederate line, Major Pyron's column, evidently reenforced from the central one, attacked fiercely Captain Downing's company, pressing it backward with the loss in killed and wounded of a large number of these skirmishers. It seems that this company moved forward in two lines, and that one of them encountered a masked cannon firing grape shot. Thereupon, the Federal troops, disturbed by these reverses, realizing that they were outnumbered by a determined foe, and expecting an immediate charge on their position, fell back about 400 yards, and formed again in line extending along the rough ledge of rocks to the north, and below Pigeon's house, and across the arroyo near it, and on the summit and nearer slope of the wooded rocky bluff to the south—all seen in the farther portion of the view of the battleground; and upon the last elevation Captain Downing's company took a new position. On its top or western slope Lieutenant Claflin's battery was stationed. In front of it Captain Ritter's battery was first placed, but soon afterwards removed to the north into the road. His support was still the company of Captain Sopris, who was joined by Captain W. F. Wilder and his men, thus far held in the rear among the reserves. The shattered company of Captain Kerber, assisted by that of the cavalry under the command of Captain Walker, occupied the extreme northern flank of the line near its former position.

As soon as Colonel Slough's forces had vacated the ridge on the eastern side of the gulch, it was taken by the Texans, who planted their artillery on it, and again opened fire on the Federals, whose batteries responded with spirit and effectiveness. The cannonading lasted three hours, and its reverberations from the high slopes of the cañon and from distant mésas were terrific. Many trees beyond the open space in the battlefield, and particularly in the defile to the east, showed for years the marks of balls, exploding shells and canister. A gun of the Texans was dismounted by a solid shot striking it in the muzzle, and another was disabled and its limber box blown to pieces by a case shot from one of Ritter's 6-pounders. Companies D and I had picked off most of the gunners, "and if there had been anybody to support Captain Downing they never would have taken their artillery from the field." Thus the Confederates were compelled to rely mainly upon their infantry and dismounted cavalry in continuing the engagement, and could hope to succeed in reaching and breaking the line of the Federals only by bold and repeated charges upon different points of it. Colonel Slough, apprehending that this plan would be adopted, withdrew a considerable portion of Ritter's supports, sending a platoon of them to the assistance of Lieutenant Kerber and Captain Walker to act as skirmishers on his right, and the rest to strengthen the opposite flank. The latter were stationed along the bluff occupied by Claflin's battery and his supports, and farther to the south on the higher ground, where now runs the railroad. This movement was made to prevent the enemy dashing past this bluff in that direction, and attacking and destroying the wagon train along the Santa Fé trail a short distance in the rear.

Captain Jacob Downing.
(From a war-time photograph loaned by him.)
On November 1, 1862, he was promoted Major of his regiment in recognition of his gallant services in the New Mexico campaign. He is still a citizen of Denver.

By this time Colonel Scurry had been reenforced by two companies of fresh troops—perhaps 125 men. He skillfully rearranged his line for another assault, again in three divisions on the ridge he had just taken. While waiting to ascertain the exact positions held the second time by the Federals under the cover of trees, behind a long adobe wall, beyond a rocky precipice, and over the top of the bluff south of the ranch, he dispatched several squads of men, one of them clothed in the uniform of the Colorado infantry, to approach this force at different points, whose fire they would thus draw upon themselves. They were easily driven back. Thereupon, he ordered the division under Major John S. Shropshire to advance "among the pines" and vigorously attack the southern wing of Colonel Slough's army. Perceiving a delay in this onset, he left his column at the center, and on reaching these troops he discovered that the major had been killed before they could be moved forward. It happened that a portion of Captain Cook's gallant company, in the charge of Lieutenant Wilson, was directly in front of this movement, and that a private by the name of George W. Pierce had darted from its ranks, shot and disarmed Major Shropshire at the head of his battalion, and taken prisoner Captain D. W. Shannon near his side. Scurry at once assumed the command and ordered a charge by the whole body, but he met with such a spirited resistance from the Federal skirmishers that he retired. Joined by his own men from the center, he renewed the charge farther down the field toward the road, and was again repulsed by the same skirmishers, assisted by the artillery in their rear and by its supports. During these charges Lieutenant-Colonel Tappan, of the Colorado volunteers, sat on his horse as coolly "loading and firing his pistols as if rabbit hunting." In the ground where these struggles occurred a great many rifle balls were embedded and found long afterward.

Majors Raguet and Pyron were sent with their commands to the north across the arroyo, up the rugged slope, and onto the summit of the low mountain range that bounds the battlefield in that direction. Colonel Slough had anticipated this movement and a subsequent one of the Texans against his position at the ranch, and he had strengthened his right flank and his center by directing other platoons of his infantry to defend the former, and by restationing his batteries where they could do better execution in the latter. Captain Ritter left the road in front of the ranch and crossed the arroyo to the opposite side of the narrow gorge. Previous to this change he had lost two trusted lieutenants who had been associated with him—Peter McGrath, of the regular cavalry, and Clark Chambers, of Company C, First Colorado, who was shot in the shoulder and in the thigh, and who died of his wounds after having lingered about a year. Lieutenant Claflin descended the bluff on the south and arranged his mountain howitzers near Ritter's guns. Two braver and more efficient officers in charge of artillery never fought

in the American army. The troops under Raguet and Pyron began
at once, from their superior position, a furious and steady onslaught,
with their rifles and heavy double-barreled shot guns, and then
rushed forward, dodging from tree to tree and from rock to rock,
until they came into close quarters with the Federals, who, deliver-
ing volley after volley, yielded the ground only inch by inch, as
they were pushed back onto the ledge of rocks that extends northward from the ranch. So near together were these contending
ranks at times that "the muzzles of their guns passed by each other
over the top of the loosened rocks," and some of them shot at each
other from opposite sides of the same clump of cedar bushes.

Colonel Scurry, aware of the decisive advantage he had gained
by this contest of his left flank, quickly united with it, near the
middle of the afternoon, his main forces from the right and the
center of his line. They made their stand at first in the road and
immediately across the arroyo, some 300 yards west of the ranch.
His aim was to capture the Federal batteries in the gorge in front
of him, and to drive the Federal skirmishers from the ledges to
which they had retired shortly before. He issued his commands
with great energy, an exceedingly resonant voice, and a clear understanding of the difficulties to be overcome. He mingled with
his troops, animating them to engage in the final and desperate
encounter of the day. Raguet and Pyron moved about everywhere
among them, inspiring the rank and file to deeds of daring and re-
nown. Possibly the fate of the whole campaign, embracing their
weary march from their distant homes and their invaluable con-
quests in the Rio Grandé valley, depended upon the results achieved
in the next three hours. Officers and men responded with alacrity
and grim determination. With the brim of their slouched hats falling over their foreheads, and with deafening yells, they charged
impetuously down the road and its sides toward Ritter's and Claflin's batteries, but were checked before reaching these by grape shot,
canister and exploding shells, and by the galling fire of the infantry
in the gorge and on the opposite elevations. Five times they
attempted the assault upon this position of the Federals, and as
many times they were repulsed. In an interval between two of

these, a German officer in the Colorado volunteers shouted in broken but emphatic English to his men standing in a huddle near the artillery: "Poys, lay down flat dere; does you vant to go died?" In at least two of these charges the Texans advanced to within forty or fifty steps of the guns. Then Claflin ordered his men to cease firing, and his supports, rising from the ground and running forward, shot their deadly rifle bullets fairly into the faces of the approaching enemy, and dashed in close rank into the wavering column, scattering it in great disorder. The fighting here was most deadly, the hottest that any of these soldiers had yet witnessed, and in it the Texans suffered severely. The accomplished Raguet, the chivalrous Captain Charles Buckholts and the brave Lieutenant Charles H. Mills fell near the same time. Colonel Scurry, who won the undisguised admiration of the Colorado volunteers for his magnificent courage and intrepid leadership, had some narrow escapes. On March 30th, when he said "I do not know if I write intelligently, for I have not slept for three nights and can scarcely hold my eyes open," he reported the battle to General Sibley, who was then on his way from Albuquerqué to Santa Fé. After referring to the death of Raguet and other officers, he went on to say: "Major Pyron had his horse shot under him, and my own cheek was twice brushed by a minie ball, each time just drawing blood, and my clothes torn in two places. I mention this simply to show how hot was the fire of the enemy when all of the field officers upon the ground were either killed or touched." In another report he said the "conflict was terrible," and that the men who opposed him were "the flower of the U. S. army."

A pathetic incident occurred in the Federal ranks in connection with the death of Major Raguet. A full-grown boy, just reaching young manhood, belonged to the Colorado volunteers. Early in the forenoon he said to Captain Downing: "I dreamed last night that I was shot through my heart in a battle to-day, and I believe it will come true." The captain cheerfully told him: "You have a mere fancy, produced by a bad dream, and you should give no heed to it." During the engagement he detailed the youth with others to conduct some prisoners back to the camp at Kozlowski's, and did

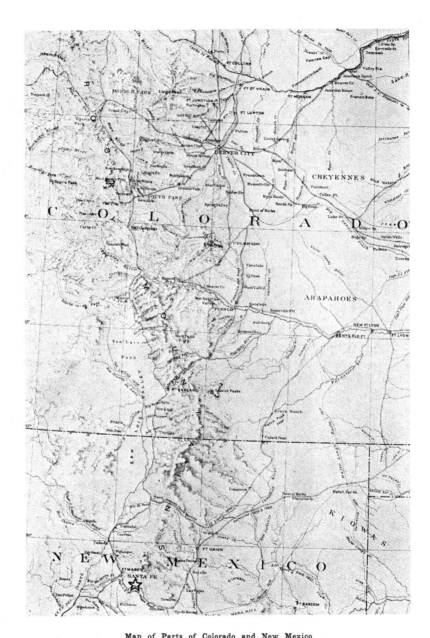

Map of Parts of Colorado and New Mexico.

(From a Military Map issued by the War Department in 1867, in the State Historical
and Natural History Society's collection.)

The star (here added to the map) near the lower left-hand corner marks the locality
of La Glorieta Pass.

not expect him to return to the battlefield. What was the captain's surprise to find him late in the afternoon in his old place among the men on a bluff at Pigeon's ranch! It was remarked to him: "If you still want to engage in the fight, take a rifle and see if you can hit that Confederate officer on horseback." The officer was about forty rods away in the field. The boy took deliberate aim and fired his gun, and Major Raguet fell from the saddle mortally wounded. A Texan sharpshooter, observing this action, instantly discharged at the boy a rifle bullet, which, striking his gun, glanced from it and pierced his heart. Turning to the captain at his side, he gasped: "I told you something would happen."

While this fight was in progress a detachment of Scurry's command gained possession of the ledges to the north, and poured a destructive fusillade into that side of the Federal batteries. These with the infantry withdrew in good order down the cañon to the rear of the open field beyond the ranch, and there formed their third position in the battle. The supply train was forty yards to their left. Captain Downing was among the last to leave his place on the bluff at the gorge, and to join in the new line of defense. Here the Texans made another, and their last, charge upon these batteries, and endeavored to reach the train, but they were again driven back with loss and in confusion.

Soon after five o'clock in the afternoon Colonel Slough ordered his forces to abandon this position and return to their camp at Kozlowski's. This was effected by the pieces of artillery and the wagons, well guarded, withdrawing one after the other. The men were enraged by this movement, and vigorously upbraided their commander, for they were eager to move upon the Confederates and complete the work of the day, either by forcing a surrender or starting them upon a retreat toward Santa Fé. But to Colonel Slough the object of the reconnoissance in force, "to annoy and harass the enemy," had been accomplished. It seems that Ritter's battery remained, in the last position where it had been stationed, for some time after the order to fall back upon the camp had passed along the line. On Captain Downing then approaching him, he said: "Captain, you are the only ranking officer left on the field.

What are your orders to me?" The quick reply was: "Double-shot your guns and keep on firing." Finding that he was not properly supported, Captain Ritter began to prepare soon after for drawing the battery off the field in the direction of the camp.

Just at that time an ambulance bearing a flag of truce was driven down the road from the west. On reaching Captains Downing and Ritter there alighted from it the assistant adjutant-general of Sibley's brigade—Major Alexander M. Jackson, the former secretary of New Mexico, an ardent secessionist, a personal friend of President Davis of the Confederacy, one of the chief instigators of General Sibley's invasion of the territory, and doubtless the one on whom the responsibility for it mainly rested. He asked for a suspension of hostilities until noon of the following day, in order that his wounded could be cared for and his dead buried. He was thrust back into his conveyance, and directed by Captain Downing to proceed blindfolded toward Kozlowski's. He did so, and met Colonel Slough, who granted his request, the armistice being subsequently extended to the morning of the second day. In fact, the troops under Lieutenant-Colonel Scurry were so exhausted and crippled by the struggle through which they had passed that they could not further continue the fighting at that juncture. The battle had lasted without interruption at least seven hours, and since early morning neither army had had any opportunity to rest and take refreshment.

In the meantime, and unknown to Colonel Slough at the time the armistice was agreed to, a crushing disaster had been inflicted upon Colonel Scurry's resources by the column under Major Chivington, which had been dispatched in the morning to the western end of the pass. This force was composed of the following named organizations: Captain W. H. Lewis' battalion (regulars), with Captain A. B. Carey assisting him in command, consisting of sixty men; Companies A and G, Fifth Regular Infantry, in charge of Lieutenants Barr and Norvell; Company B, First regiment Colorado Volunteers, seventy-eight men, in charge of Captain Samuel M. Logan and Lieutenant Jacobs; Ford's independent company of Colorado Volunteers, in charge of Captain James H. Ford and Lieutenant DeForrest; Captain E. W. Wynkoop's battalion, consisting of Company A, First Colorado, sixty-eight men, under Lieutenant Shaffer; Company E, First Colorado, seventy-one men, under Captain Scott J. Anthony and Lieutenant Dawson, and Company H, First Colorado, about eighty men, under Captain George L. Sanborn and Lieutenant Sanford; in all, "about 430 officers and picked men." Lieutenant-Colonel Manuel Chavis, of the New Mexico Volunteers, was selected as the guide, and it was expected that the reconnoissance around over the mountains to Johnson's ranch would be exceedingly toilsome and dangerous. Colonel Chavis was a member of an old and distinguished Mexican family in the territory; had taken part in the Mexican War with Governor Gilpin of Colorado; had won honors in skirmishes with the Apache Indians; had fought under Colonel Canby at Valverdé, and was a brave, loyal and skillful officer.

This column marched past the ruins of the Pécos pueblo, and left the main road about a mile to the west, where a trail branches off and goes through the San Cristobal cañon to Galistéo. While following this for eight miles the troops heard the discharges of the artillery at Pigeon's ranch, and knew that fighting had begun there in earnest. A mounted company was sent to scout in that direction, in order to warn them, if necessary, after they had left the Galistéo trail and turned to the right toward Johnson's ranch, of the approach of any Confederate force in their rear. Leaving this trail, they made their way eight miles farther, over rocks, up steep ascents, and through dense thickets of scrub piñon and cedar bushes, to the crest of a mountain that immediately overlooked the Texan encampment. Here they arrived between one and two o'clock in the afternoon, having been five hours on the march, and here they captured a sentinel, who had been stationed on this height by Colonel Scurry. Colonel Chavis, looking down more than a thousand feet on the camp, with its accessories, and the troops and teamsters in charge of it—about 250 men, all told—remarked to Major Chivington: "You are right on top of them." An hour was spent in carefully examining the situation below, and wholly unobserved by the enemy. The ranch house was in plain view, as were the adobe huts near it, the road leading from the cañon just north of

View of the Precipitous Mountainside Descended by Major Chivington's Command at Johnson's Ranch, or Canoncito.

(From one of the author's photographs.)

them to Santa Fé, the ravines reaching out to the right and to the left, the abrupt knolls in different places, a mounted cannon on the highest of these, the wagons and some draft animals in a group at the center, and the soldiers leisurely moving about.

The illustration, showing the mountainside descended by Major Chivington's force when the camp was attacked, was taken from the summit of an oblong knoll rising fully 150 feet, between which and the mountains is a deep and very narrow defile. Through this defile runs the track of the Santa Fé Railway, and in it lies somewhat hidden the base of the highest mountain. Immediately to the left of the lower one, which is partially seen in the view, is the western opening of La Gloriéta pass. It was upon the summit of the central mountain that Major Chivington made his observations, and it was down the steep slope of that mountain that he led his men upon the unsuspecting guardians of the camp.

Having satisfied himself that no formidable difficulty existed to prevent an attack upon the encampment, he gave the order to his men: "In single file, double-quick, charge!" Instantly they were on the brow of the steep cliff, and soon on their way down it, being lowered at first by ropes, leathern straps, and by holding on with their guns and to each other, and at length, by crawling, sliding and leaping down the lower half of the slope, they reached the bottom. When they had completed a fourth of their descent, the crashing of loosened rocks down the precipice and among the small trees aroused the attention of the troops in the camp. Soon eight gunners on the knoll began firing shots from their 6-pounder into the descending and scattered companies, but without effect. Chivington's men, yelling and whooping like wild Indians, were not long in reaching the base of the mountain, where they formed themselves again into ranks. At once some of the frightened teamsters and infantrymen on guard seized the horses and mules at hand, and scampered away and disappeared up the road toward Santa Fé, while many others retreated at double-quick into the cañon running eastward. It is not difficult to account for the almost defenseless condition of the encampment. The flank movement of Major Chivington's troops was not anticipated in the least by Colonel Scurry.

Beside, when he left in the morning, he detached a much larger force to protect his supplies and animals here than the one found by the Federals upon their arrival. The writer while in New Mexico was told by a Texas captain, past middle age, that he was placed in command of this camp on the departure of Scurry, and that two companies of Germans were, with others, assigned him to care for its valuable stores and other property. These Germans, on hearing the booming of the cannon at Pigeon's ranch, declared that they had "enlisted to get glory by fighting, and not in guarding mules and provisions." It was impossible for him to restrain them, and so, breaking away from their comrades, they hastened through the cañon and joined the other troops on the field of battle. These were the reenforcements that Colonel Scurry received about the middle of the afternoon.

Major Chivington, not aware of the small number of men at the camp, and fearing an ambuscade, arranged at first his companies in order of battle near the ranch, and had them march and counter-march so as to be ready to resist an attack, if such should be attempted by any force concealed somewhere in the vicinity. He soon learned that there was no ground for his fears. Then Captain Wynkoop was dispatched with thirty of his men, under an order to silence the gun on the high knoll, the discharges of which thus far had proved harmless. In closer quarters, however, the gun might be destructive. Three of those handling it were instantly killed, and several were wounded, by a single volley from the rifles of Wynkoop's men. Major Chivington then divided his troops into two columns, one directed to take possession of the knoll and to capture the piece of artillery on its top, and the other to capture and hold the supply train in the corral. The first of these movements, the more daangerous one, was executed under the charge of Captain Lewis. Assisted by Lieutenant B. N. Sanford, of Captain George L. Sanborn's company, he ascended this knoll, spiked the cannon with a steel ramrod, jammed a 6-pound iron ball into its muzzle, and tumbled the carriage upon which it was mounted down the eastern side of the knoll, smashing the wheels into pieces. Beside this, they set fire to a quantity of ammunition designed for this gun and hidden, a limber box, covered over with brush and dirt, in a small gully on the opposite side of this knoll.   In this exploit the lieutenant came dangerously near losing his life.   They also searched the buildings and the ravines roundabout for concealed Texans, of whom they made prisoners of several.

The other column charged upon and surrounded the wagon train, meeting with no serious opposition.   It consisted of heavily loaded wagons, more often estimated to be seventy-three in number.   In them were ammunition, subsistence, forage, baggage, officers' clothing, medical and surgical stores—all of the equipage and other necessary supplies for a small army in camp and on the march.   Under the circumstances, nothing from this great quantity of stores could well be conveyed away by the captors.   To destroy them utterly, so that they could not be used by the invaders, was considered the only course left to be pursued.   All of the wagons, most of them hastily overturned, were burned with their entire contents.   In one case bacon and cavalry saddles had been piled upon boxes of powder, and the explosion of the latter sent portions of both the former about 200 feet up into the air.   In another instance the ammunition exploded in the midst of burning other articles, severely wounding Private Ritter, of Wynkoop's company—the only man hurt in the expedition.   All of the materials belonging to the wagons, except their iron work, were consumed.   Some extracts from a letter written by one of General Sibley's men to his wife have appeared on a preceding page.   In referring to the destruction of the wagon train, he says: "Our whole train of eighty-five wagons was burned by the enemy.   In one of these was that trunk of clothing you sent me at Fort Fillmore.   It was burned with the rest."   He was compelled to rely upon the charity of those who held him as a prisoner for his needed apparel in the succeeding months of his stay in the territory.   While the troops were watching the smoldering ruins of the train, a Confederate messenger on horseback dashed out of the ravine back of the ranch house, turned suddenly into the mouth of the cañon, and rode at the top of his horse's speed toward Pigeon's ranch, where the fighting between the forces of Slough and Scurry was still raging.   It is very probable that the information he gave to Colonel Scurry occasioned the sending of the flag of truce to Colonel Slough just before nightfall that day.

There remained another serious damage to be inflicted upon the property of the Confederates in the camp—all that was left of any value. The animals—horses and mules—ridden here by officers and some of the privates of the army were found corraled in an

Main Building and Corral at Johnson's Ranch, Where the Confederate Encampment and Wagon-Train Were Destroyed by Major Chivington's Detachment.
(From one of the author's photographs.)

arm of a deep ravine about half a mile away. Estimates of their number varied considerably, but the most trustworthy made it between 500 and 600. They could not be removed over the mountains to the Federal camp, and so they were all bayoneted. A soldier who was present said of this: "It seemed a pity to kill them, but we could do nothing else with them." If permitted to live, they would be used by their owners in protracting the campaign. As to this loss of the Texans, the writer of the letter from which I have heretofore quoted remarked: "It went hard with the boys to walk, as we were all well mounted when we came to this country." Five Union soldiers who had been captured by Scurry and sent to the camp as prisoners were released by Chivington's force. They gave a doleful account, colored by its consequences to them, of the state of affairs back at Pigeon's ranch. Seventeen Confederates, two of them being officers, were captured by Chivington's troops and taken away prisoners. A rumor prevailed among the Federals before they left the wrecked camp that a heavy reenforcement, then due, was rapidly approaching from Galistéo, the former encampment of the Confederates, and, therefore, it was decided not to march back to Kozlowski's by way of the pass, but by the route they had followed in coming, and thus to avoid the danger of being caught in a trap between two divisions of the enemy.

It was almost night when this force on the return had climbed to the summit of the mountain, the precipitous slope of which had been descended only a few hours before. On the way up it was noticed that four wagons, filled with military stores, were hidden behind a knoll outside of the main camp, and had been overlooked in the work of destruction. Four men volunteered to go back and burn them, and accomplished their task within an hour.

Major Chivington on this summit was met by a lieutenant with orders from Colonel Slough to hasten back with his command to Camp Lewis at Kozlowski's, and to unite them with the division which had withdrawn from Pigeon's ranch that evening. Some time was spent in parleying as to what route should be taken. Colonel Chavis was unwilling to take the responsibility of serving as guide on any way other than the one followed in coming. At this point in the deliberation, a Mexican Catholic priest on a milk-white horse, and who is now known to have been Padré Ortiz, from a small hamlet near the Pécos ruin, rode into their midst and saluted the officers in Spanish. He offered to lead them to their camp over the mountains alongside the pass and by a shorter course, and warned them that if they returned by the old trail they would doubtless meet with some of Scurry's troops, and have trouble in the night. Chavis was acquainted with this priest, understood what he said, and advised Chivington to accept his services. In intense darkness, over steep ridges, through narrow defiles, and along a pathless route, he conducted the column in safety to the main road near the old Pécos pueblo, where the troops had turned into the Galistéo trail in the morning. Somewhere near this place they halted, fearing that the enemy might be in the vicinity and would attack them under the cover of the night. But they remained here only a few minutes, having failed to discover any cause for alarm. Soon after, by ten o'clock, Chivington's force, weary, suffering intensely from thirst, and apprehensive that the events of the day at Pigeon's ranch had resulted disastrously to the other division, rejoined their comrades from whom they had separated in the morning, who joyously welcomed the victors and eagerly listened to the account of their achievements.

Vallé, the "Pigeon" of the noted ranch, was an eye-witness of the battle fought on and around his property, and excitedly, but briefly, described it thus: "Ze Tex mahns coom oop und zoorbrize zem [the Federals] und zay foight zeex 'ourz by my vatch; und ze vatch vas zlow."

Available official and other reports of the losses by both Union and Confederate forces in the two engagements in La Gloriéta pass —which really constituted one battle—are, as to the former, to some extent conflicting, and as to the latter greatly at variance. The killed and wounded on the Union side evidently exceeded the number stated in the official reports. Before he slept, after the fight in Apache cañon, Major Chivington wrote his report of that affair to "Brig. Gen. [Colonel] E. R. S. Canby," in which he said "our loss was five killed and fourteen wounded." Colonel Slough, in reporting the second conflict to Colonel Canby, under date March 29th, gave his loss in killed as "probably twenty; in wounded probably fifty." In his report of March 30th, to the adjutant-general of the army, at Washington, of the second battle, he made this statement: "Our loss is not great. We have 1 officer (Lieutenant Baker, Colorado Volunters) killed, and 2 (Lieutenant McGrath, United States army, and Lieutenant Chambers, Colorado Volunteers) wounded; 28 men killed and 40 wounded. We lost some fifteen prisoners." Lieutenant-Colonel Tappan, in a report of the second fight, made May 31st, said: "I was assigned to the immediate command of a battalion of infantry, consisting of Companies

C, Captain Sopris; D, Captain Downing; G, Captain Wilder; I, Captain Mailie, and K, Captain Robbins, First Colorado Volunteers. A battery of four guns—two 12-pounders and two 6-pounders, Captain Ritter, regular army, and four 12-pounder mountain howitzers, Lieutenant Claflin, United States regular army, were attached to my command. * * * An estimate was made after the battle of the casualties of my command, and, if my memory serves me, 29 killed, 64 wounded, and 13 missing." Governor Connelly, writing to the secretary of state, at Washington, on March 30th, informed him that "our loss in killed, wounded and missing in the two days' encounter will reach 150." A statement of the losses among the Colorado Volunteers, giving the names of their killed and wounded during this history-making campaign, probably not accurate in every particular, but as nearly so as can be ascertained at this time, appears on later pages of this volume. There it may be seen that the casualties of the Colorado Volunteers, alone, exceeded the totals of the officers' reports quoted above; yet, as the reader knows, there were some other Union troops which fought in the engagements in La Gloriéta pass.

Dr. Lewis C. Tolles, Assistant-Surgeon of the First Colorado Regiment.

(From a war-time photograph in the State Historical and Natural History Society's collection.

As to the Confederates' losses, the exact truth is not likely ever to be known. No report of theirs of their killed and wounded in Apache cañon could be found. Major Chivington informed Colonel Canby, March 26th, that "the loss of the enemy was, as we ascertained from their own accounts, 32 killed, 43 wounded, and 71 taken prisoners." Of their misfortunes in the second fight, Colonel Slough, in his report of March 29th to Colonel Canby, said: "The enemy's loss is in killed from 40 to 60, and in wounded probably over 100. In addition, we took some 25 prisoners." Reporting to the adjutant-general of the army on March 30th, Slough wrote: "The loss of the enemy is great. His killed amount to at least 100, his wounded at least 150. * * * He is still burying his dead. It is claimed that in the battles of the 26th and 28th together we damaged the enemy at least 350 killed, wounded and prisoners." On March 30th the governor of New Mexico, who was one of Secretary Seward's most active correspondents, reported to that member of the cabinet that the Confederate losses were "fully double the number" of those of the Union forces. On April 6th he sent word to Mr. Seward that "the loss of the enemy in the late encounter does not fall short of 400 men in killed, wounded and missing;" and added that "near 200" Confederate wounded were still at the battlefield. Over seventy dead bodies of Confederate soldiers were said to have been seen the day after the second fight lying on the earthen floor of the largest apartment in Vallé's house (Pigeon's ranch), gathered from the battlefield and awaiting burial. It was also said that among their belongings which the Confederates afterward left behind them at Albuquerqué were some of their records, including those of their surgeons, and that according to these their losses in the two fights in La Gloriéta pass were 281 killed and 200 wounded. But this story about the surgeons' books was never satisfactorily authenticated.

However, it is very close to the facts to say that the Union losses in killed and wounded in Colonel Slough's force on March 28th was about one-fourth of the number of troops engaged; and that the Confederates lost in the two fights more than one-fourth of their men who entered the pass. Their officers were remarkably unfortunate, for, as we have seen, Colonel Scurry reported that all of his field officers "upon the ground were either killed or touched."

Most of the Union dead of the second fight were interred in the open field to the east of Pigeon's ranch, and by the side of those who had fallen two days before in the Apache cañon. The Confederate dead were laid side by side in a great trench excavated in a level spot across the arroyo, just west of the ranch, and close to the high ledge of rocks. A long and slight depression in the ground marks to-day their resting place—their undisturbed and final bivouac.

It was, indeed, a stunning, fatal blow that Chivington's force had inflicted at Johnson's ranch, not only upon the rear, but upon the advance of Scurry's army, and also upon the entire campaign of the Confederates in the Southwest. This rear was utterly scattered and ruined, and further advance was made hopeless. The Texans, after staying at Pigeon's ranch two days and two nights subsequent to the second battle, without shelter or blankets, and practically without food, retreated to Santa Fé in search of provisions, leaving at the ranch their wounded, mentioned by Governor Connelly as being nearly 200 in number. Of ammunition they had remaining, on an average, no more than ten rounds for each small firearm, and were almost without any for their artillery. They could not have renewed the engagement, as Colonel Slough had expected them to do at the time the truce was arranged; nor could they have made much resistance to an attack from Slough, had he attempted to intercept their retreat to Santa Fé immediately upon the termination of the truce. The effect upon Sibley, who had hurried to Santa Fé from Albuquerqué, and upon those of his advisers who had participated in the fight, was shown in the decision soon reached by him and them, that they had utterly failed to attain the object of their operations in New Mexico, and that the skeleton of their army must return to Texas with all practicable speed.

It is worthy of note, in passing, that among Colonel Scurry's soldiers at La Gloriéta was Private Joseph D. Sayres, who, at the time of this writing, is governor of the great and prosperous state of Texas.

Colonel Slough's troops, after burying their dead, and removing their wounded to Kozlowski's ranch, which then became a crowded hospital, started for Fort Union in the afternoon of March 30th, the second day after their memorable struggle with the Texans at La Gloriéta. They had received positive instructions from Colonel Canby to fall back to that post, in order to protect it "at all hazards, and to leave nothing to chance." The fear was entertained that a detachment of the Confederates, pursuing some other route, would endeavor to surprise and take it. On the sixth day thereafter the governor of the territory wrote to Washington that had they, instead of going on this march, advanced immediately after the battle toward Santa Fé, "it would have led to the entire capture or dispersion of the enemy's force." When the troops arrived at Fort Union they found that it was not in the remotest danger of being attacked. By the end of ten days after leaving Kozlowski's they encamped near there again, under orders to hasten to the aid of Colonel Canby's small army near Albuquerqué, which had left Fort Craig on the first of April. In the meantime, Colonel Slough, disgusted because he had not been permitted to follow up the advantages that had been gained at La Gloriéta and effect the capture or dispersion of Colonel Scurry's force, resigned his commission. In the feeling of exasperation that led to this, his officers and men sympathized with him.

Hollister, from whom I have once before quoted, in his historical pamphlet says of Colonel Slough, in connection with the failure to pursue the demoralized Confederates:

"Flushed with an honorable and complete victory, his brave troops eager to complete the destruction of the enemy, Colonel Slough read the despatch brought by Captain Nicodemus, in dismay. He could not destroy the order; it had been too openly delivered to leave any room for evasion. To obey it was to let the enemy, broken and disheartened, escape; to refuse was to subject himself to court martial and disgrace.

"He issued the order for the backward movement, but resigned his commission. * * *."

Colonel Slough later went to Washington and was commissioned in the spring of 1863 a brigadier-general by President Lincoln, and placed in command of the Military District of Alexandria, Virginia. He survived the war, and after its close was appointed chief justice of the territory of New Mexico.

PRECIPITATE RETREAT OF THE CONFEDERATES FROM NEW MEXICO.

Before Colonel Canby ordered the main force, including the Colorado Volunteers, at Fort Union to proceed at once to join him in the Rio Grandé valley, he had formed a plan to drive, if possible, the remnants of General Sibley's forces out of New Mexico. He selected 1,200 of his troops, largely regulars, at Fort Craig. for an expedition north under his command, placing Colonel Kit Carson, with ten companies of New Mexico Volunteers, in charge of the post during his absence. He decided to march northward until he could be joined by reenforcements from Fort Union, and then with the two columns united compel Sibley to withdraw from Santa Fé.

But the Confederates already had some plans of their own, having resolved to withdraw, not only from Santa Fé, but from the territory itself, and to do so without waiting for any more force to be applied to them. Immediately after the battle of La Gloriéta they began preparations for their retreat down the Rio Grandé valley into Texas. On the 5th and 6th of April they evacuated Santa Fé and marched for Albuquerqué, leaving behind them all of their sick and wounded who were unable to take some care of themselves.

General Sibley had succeeded in occupying what is now Old Albuquerqué before Colonel Canby and his troops from Fort Craig arrived in the vicinity on the 8th of April. The former had stationed his artillery at different points in the town, and strongly at Armijo's mill in the eastern end, which is now a residence portion, called Gloriéta.

Colonel Canby soon planted his battery about a mile to the east of the mill in a large irrigating ditch, at the place where are now located the water works of the new town, more spacious by far than the old one, and he arranged here the supports of his four guns along in the ditch and behind a low embankment on its west side.

The hostile forces were engaged for about two days in artillery duels from the points already described, and in sharp skirmishing on the borders of the town. The destruction of property and the casualties among the men on both sides were slight. Canby sought to discover more fully the strength and intentions of the Confederates, and the latter aimed to conceal these, and to prevent the capture of the supplies they had collected. The former made a request for the women and children to be removed from the town,

View in Old Albuquerque in the Late Fifties.
(From a wood engraving in "El Gringo," by W. W. H. Davis, 1857.)

and upon this being refused, he ceased to bombard it, and retired in the night northeastward toward Sandia mountain, and entered the Carnuél cañon, which cuts through the center of it, and camped finally at Tijéras, about fifteen miles from Albuquerqué. Here he awaited the coming of the troops from Fort Union. They reached him late in the evening of the 13th of April, having marched through a rough pass and over a high mésa, and on the last day, forty-six miles, losing by death many of their horses and mules, and leaving some of the men exhausted on the route.

General Sibley, not fearing any further attack at Albuquerqué, for a few days, soon completed his arrangements to evacuate the place and to continue what he called "this retrograde movement."

9

Here, then, was the depot of all of his supplies. He buried here, as he had at Santa Fé, a part of the brass cannon with which his command originally had been provided, retaining their carriages for transportation purposes, but he held on to the six field pieces he had captured from Canby at Valverdé. By this time ammunition for the guns he buried had been entirely exhausted.

On the 12th of April the main portion of the Confederate troops crossed the Rio Grandé near Albuquerqué, and proceeded down the west bank to Los Lunas, where they were ordered to wait for the arrival of the remainder. On the morrow the latter marched down on the eastern side of the river about twenty miles to the ranch of Territorial Governor Connelly, and occupied his spacious residence, situated in "quite a dense forest of trees," and at a short distance from Péralta, nearly opposite Los Lunas. The farming lands of the place were enclosed by high adobe walls, affording a defense like a fortification. Here this force remained almost two days.

The resignation of Colonel Slough having taken effect on April 9th, a petition, signed by all of the other officers of the First Colorado, asking that Major Chivington be promoted his successor, was presented to Colonel Canby by Lieutenant-Colonel Tappan upon the arrival of the regiment at the latter's camp at Tijéras in the evening of April 13th. By a field order dated April 14th Canby made the appointment. Virtually from the first, because of his presence, popularity and superior ability, Chivington had been the regiment's real leader.

In the morning of April 14th Colonel Canby's command left Tijéras, and after a march of thirty-six miles southward went into camp in the evening of that day, without the enemy's knowledge, about a mile from Governor Connelly's ranch, where the Confederates, in that pleasant refuge, were enjoying with music and dancing a careless "revelry by night." Colonel Chivington and his men insisted upon attacking them at once, surprising and capturing them, and so ending the career of this divsion of Sibley's shattered and demoralized forces before they slept. Canby refused the necessary permission, saying a night attack was generally disastrous to the party making it, and intimating that he preferred the enemy should flee out of the country seeking their own supplies, than for him to capture them and be compelled to furnish their subsistence from his insufficient stores.   For this the feeling against him became extremely bitter, and the suspicion was entertained that, since he was

Present Appearance of the Site of the Armijo Mill in Old Albuquerque.
(From one of the author's photographs.)

a brother-in-law to General Sibley, he was disposed to injure his own cause by favoring that of the latter.

Early next morning a train of seven wagons loaded with supplies and accompanied by a mountain howitzer, in charge of a Confederate officer and thirty men, was discovered approaching from Albuquerqué.   A detachment of the Federals hastened to attack the escort.   In the fight that followed six of the enemy were killed, three wounded, and the latter, with all of the others, were made prisoners, and the train and the howitzer brought into camp.   In the forenoon Colonel Canby moved upon the Confederates and drove them from Governor Connelly's ranch some distance toward the river and into another bosqué, where they were joined during the day by reenforcements from their main column, that had halted

at Los Lunas, on the other side of the stream. Skirmishing and
cannonading between the opposing forces were continued until
after nightfall, with the advantages on the Federal side. Aside
from those killed and wounded in the capture of the wagon train,
nothing definite is known of the Confederate losses at Péralta.
Colonel Canby reported that the Union side had one killed and
three wounded, but none taken prisoner. Colonel Chivington and
one of his captains barely escaped a cannon ball, which, after skip-
ping along the ground directly toward them, bounded a few inches
over their heads. The tragic incident is told of two Federal soldiers,
walking near these officers over the ground raked by the Confederate guns, being fatally struck in their bodies by the same ball.

Here, in this engagement at Péralta, on the 15th of April, the
Confederates fired their last shot at Union soldiers in General Sibley's ill-fated campaign in New Mexico, for Colonel Canby permitted them to escape from the territory without further molesta-
tion from him, "although his force was double that of Sibley." At
ten o'clock that night their troops which had been in the fight of
the day, withdrew from their position and began in dense darkness
to cross the Rio Grandé at Los Lunas, leaving behind their dead,
and some wounded and sick, and by next morning the reunited
columns had advanced five miles down the west side of the stream
in their retreat. This movement was made "with the full knowledge
of Colonel Canby," as stated in a published article written by an
officer in his confidence. For this and for his subsequent conduct
in the "pursuit" of General Sibley's broken command, in which there
was or seemed to be a willingness to permit the Confederates to go
in peace, the Union people of New Mexico, as well as nearly all of
his soldiers, never forgave Colonel Canby.

It was alleged in behalf of Canby that it was impossible for the
Union troops to cross the river as the enemy had done and follow
them along the same bank, because the spring rains had greatly
swollen the stream, and that the only ferry boat in that vicinity had
been sunk by those using it the night before. So Canby undertook the "race" after the Confederates on the east side, the two
commands being nearly opposite each other on the 16th and 17th,

and frequently within the easy range of their cannon. On the evening of the 17th they went into camp with the river between them, and each plainly in sight of the other. In the morning of the 18th Canby discovered that the enemy had disappeared before daylight, although some of their camp fires, which had been abundantly replenished at the time of going, still were burning. The Confederates had abandoned a purpose they formed while on this retreat to move rapidly on Fort Craig, "attack its weak garrison and

The Ditch in Front of the Albuquerque Water Works, in Which Colonel Canby Planted
His Artillery.
(From one of the author's photographs.)

demolish the fort," as a farewell performance, and, instead of this, they had suddenly decided to take a more difficult and hazardous route, twenty miles farther to the west, through the San Matéo mountains, and to return to the river at a point thirty miles below Fort Craig, near Alamosa. So, at a short distance to the southwest of Socorro, and during a terrific wind and sand storm, such as does not often visit New Mexico, they diverged to this course before daybreak of the 18th, packing most of the supplies they took with them on mules. They left at their camp some sick and wounded, whom Canby reported as found "without attendance, without medicines, and almost without food," and also "thirty-six wagons and the supplies that they contained," together with a miscellaneous lot of impedimenta. They had stripped themselves to the limit for their most toilsome march, which they were ten days in making, meanwhile enduring actual suffering from lack of food and much hardship in an extremely rough and desolate region. But they avoided the possibility of another encounter with the Union troops, especially with the disappointed Colorado Volunteers, who longed to administer upon them a blow that would destroy their organization.

Of the march of the Confederates on this detour an officer who served with Colonel Canby, in an account of this campaign, says:

"Sibley's retreat was a most desperate one. He passed on the west side of the Sierra Madélena, through the Sierra dé San Matéo, until he reached the dry bed of the Rio Palomas, down which he continued until he reached the Rio Grandé, where supplies had been sent from Mésilla to meet him. His command was entirely worn out and nearly famished. This distance from where he left the Rio Grandé until he reached it again was over one hundred

Map Showing the Detour-route Followed by General Sibley on His Retreat from New Mexico.
(From "Battles and Leaders of the Civil War." The Century Company, 1887.)

miles, and the Confederates were ten days accomplishing this distance, with five days of poor rations. The route was through the worst country in that territory, with no guides, trail or road. What artillery they got through with was dragged up hill and lowered by the men, who used long ropes for that purpose. The undergrowth and brush were so dense that for several miles they were forced to cut their way through with axes and bowie knives. Nearly all of the ammunition was abandoned on the way, as was nearly everything else, except what the men carried upon their persons. On passing over the route of these unfortunate men, nearly a year after, I not infrequently found a piece of a gun carriage, or part of a harness, or some piece of camp or garrison equipage, with occasionally a white, dry skeleton of a man. At some points it seemed impossible for men to have made their way. During this retreat the Confederates were unmolested by the Union troops, with the exception of the ubiquitous Captain Graydon, who with his [independent spy] company followed them alone for a long distance, picking up a large amount of serviceable articles, which they had abandoned on the way."

In a report to the adjutant-general of the army, at Washington, dated May 4th, Colonel Canby said:

"Scouts and prisoners report this force as greatly demoralized, and that they have abandoned everything that could impede their flight. Sick and wounded have been left by the wayside, without care and often without food. Many of them have been collected and are properly cared for, and arrangements have been made to bring in the others and secure any valuable property that has been abandoned by the enemy."

After sending some men to collect and care for the property the Confederates had abandoned at their camp, Canby had continued his march on the east side of the river to Polvadéra, where he crossed. Here he rested his men for a day, and then resumed his leisurely way down to Fort Craig, where he arrived on the 22d of April. There, for the next six weeks, the men half starved, each with the allowance of only six ounces of flour daily, while waiting for a train loaded with the needed supplies to arrive from the North, and which was detained by the severe rains and the overflow of the river that prevailed during the time. To their great surprise, the first that arrived consisted only of vinegar and whiskey—not an ounce of provisions.

By the beginning of May General Sibley had distributed what remained of his forces in the villages along the Rio Grandé from Doña Aña to El Paso. Colonel Canby reported to the secretary of war that the Confederate commander had left behind him, "in dead and wounded, and in sick, prisoners and missing, one-half of his original force." Only seven wagons were brought back, while 327 were reported as taken northward by him from Mésilla five months previous, and the only artillery he had was McRae's battery of six guns, captured at Valverdé. In a long report, written at Fort Bliss, Texas, May 4th, to the adjutant and inspector-general of the Confederacy, at Richmond, and giving a history of his costly campaign, General Sibley remarked: "But, sir, I can not speak encouragingly for the future; my troops having manifested a dogged, irreconcilable detestation of the country and the people." Near the close of that month he wrote to the Confederate general commanding the Western District of Texas, that provisions, forage, ammunition and clothing for his troops were "completely exhausted," and that he had "no means of renewing the supply." The financial credit of his government had declined so greatly in the valley that the Confederate paper currency had then, in 1862, the purchasing power of only twenty cents on the dollar. Early in May Lieutenant-Colonel Scurry had arrived at San Antonio, Texas, and given a full account of the disastrous campaign.

With the crushing defeat of the main Confederate movement into New Mexico, under General Sibley, and the advance of a body of Union troops from California, Military Governor Baylor's "territory of Arizona" collapsed early in the summer of 1862. He had conducted his operations with great vigor and unvarying success, and had expected soon to move upon some point at Pacific tidewater, and there establish a Confederate post and port of entry. Intelligence of the disaster to Sibley was delayed in reaching Colonel Baylor, but before the close of July all of his troops had followed those of Sibley into Texas, and New Mexico was not again troubled or entered by the Confederates during the war. Many of the men of the territory who were in sympathy with the Southern cause departed when Sibley's and Baylor's forces were driven out, to become more closely identified elsewhere with the Confederacy and its purposes.

The cannon abandoned and buried at Santa Fé by General Sibley had not, at last accounts, been recovered; but those similarly disposed of by him at Albuquerqué, eight in number, were dug up in 1892, in a garden that in 1862 was a corral, north not far from the

The Garden in Old Albuquerque Where Eight of General Sibley's Cannon Were Exhumed.
(From one of the author's photographs.)

plaza, their place of concealment having been pointed out by Major T. T. Teel, who had directed their burial, and who visited Albuquerqué in that year for the purpose of aiding in their resurrection. Four of these guns are still kept in Albuquerqué, and the other four were transferred in 1898 to the state of Colorado by the United States, and are on exhibition in the capitol at Denver, with many other relics of the Civil War, in the headquarters there of the Department of Colorado and Wyoming, Grand Army of the Republic. They are all 12-pound howitzers, and were part of the artillery which General David E. Twiggs, of the United States army, surrendered in February, 1861, at San Antonio, to Texas, on its secession from the Union. For the four which are now in the possession of Colorado that state is indebted chiefly to the efforts of Captain Cecil A. Deane, of Denver, and a veteran of the War for the Union.   While custodian of the collection of war relics in the state capitol he learned of the recovery of the eight guns, and after about six years of persistent effort, in which he was finally assisted by Honorable John F. Shafroth, then the member of congress from the Denver district, he succeeded in having the custody of four of them granted to Colorado by the war department, like authority being at the same time given to New Mexico to retain the remaining four.   After receiving the guns, and when he was cleaning them, Custodian Deane found in one of them the rust-eaten remains of a charge of canister, which had been loaded into the piece, perhaps at the battle of La Gloriéta.

Of the further history of the guns that formed McRae's battery, Captain Deane supplied me with the information embodied in this paragraph, and which he received personally from Major T. T. Teel, at El Paso, shortly before the death of that brave and chivalrous Confederate soldier.   The battery comprised four 12-pound and two 6-pound brass guns, and, as I have stated on an earlier page, they were turned, immediately after their capture, upon the Union troops at Valverdé.   In the subsequent fighting farther north they were so used again.   Because of the desperate struggle over them at the time of their capture, General Sibley's defeated and impoverished men dragged them back to Texas, even after all their other artillery had been abandoned.   Five of the guns were used by General "Dick" Taylor until the close of the war, and then were thrown into the Red river, in the bed of which they remain to this day.   At the time of the battery's capture the axle of one of the guns had been weakened by a round shot, and when those of Sibley's men who had the battery in charge reached El Paso they left the injured gun in that city, where it is still preserved—a treasured memento of men who knew not fear.   Upon its upper surface, at the breech and on that of its muzzle, discolorations, which no man would remove, are yet plainly seen.   "These," said Major Teel to Captain Deane, as the two stood by the piece of artillery, "were made by the blood of McRae and Lockridge, both of whose bodies

Four of the Brass Howitzers Buried by General Sibley at Albuquerque, While on His Retreat Down the Rio Grande Valley.

(From a photograph of the guns, which are now in the War-relic Department of the Headquarters of the Grand Army of the Republic, Department of Colorado and Wyoming, in the Capitol at Denver.)

The guns are thirty-eight inches long and of four and one-half inches calibre.

sank and rested across this gun." In a story that has long been extant, it is told that "each of these officers died at the hand of the other." Major Teel, some years before his death, publicly corrected this. He said that there was no duel, or personal encounter, between McRae and Lockridge at the gun, and that after the Confederates had removed the body of McRae they found all of the chambers of his revolver freshly loaded.

About the first of May Colonel Canby placed Colonel Chivington with his regiment, in charge of Fort Craig, as well as in command of the Southern District of New Mexico, where he and the First Colorado remained until early in July, Canby, with his staff and all of the regular troops at Fort Craig, then proceeding to the head-quarters of the department at Santa Fé. In this time Colonel Chivington dispatched four companies of his regiment to Mésilla, to welcome and protect the arrival of the advance guard of 1,800 troops, known as the "California Column," under the command of Brigadier-General James H. Carleton, who was then on an expedition from the Golden state, by way of Yuma and Tucson, to the Rio Grandé valley. He had been sent to assist in expelling the Confederate forces from New Mexico, and, if necessary, to intercept their approach to southern California. On the withdrawal of the Colorado Volunteers from the territory, his army could be distributed to points in it already abandoned by the Texans, and thus prevent any further invasion of it, and foster among the inhabitants the spirit of loyalty to the Union. This march was made in the dryest time which the arid region he crossed had experienced in thirty years, and it could easily have been interrupted by an active and determined foe, on hand at various points on the way, in attacking the very small detachments sent forward separately by General Carleton on the deserts, so that each of these could be supplied with a sufficient, though limited, quantity of water at each living spring, while any two of them often were many miles apart.

Other important results, beside driving the Texans back into their own state, had been attained by the Colorado Volunteers and detachments of the regular army, for both New Mexico and the general government, by the victory of La Gloriéta, and by their subsequent operations farther south in the Rio Grandé valley.   A large guard from this force had reoccupied Santa Fé, the capital, early in April, immediately after its evacuation by the Confederates, and were "received with public demonstrations of joy."   The people of the town, with numerous other citizens of the territory, were grateful for the relief afforded them from the depredations of a hostile army, and became more firmly attached to the cause of the Union. The territorial officers, who had been compelled to find safety in other places two months before, when the invaders were approaching Santa Fé, returned by the middle of April, reoccupied their quarters in the old "Palace," and took up the work of restoring order in the country.

Whatever indications existed among the Mormons in Utah and elsewhere, and among the Indian tribes of the Southwest, of favoring the Confederacy, were rudely checked and held in full restraint. The "malignant element" in Colorado was completely quieted; and only once thereafter during the great and long conflict for the Union was any portion of that territory alarmed or disturbed by hostile inroads from the Confederacy, and that was in 1864, when a troop of Texan guerrillas, coming from the southeast, penetrated beyond Cañon City on their way to plunder in the South Park country.   But they were soon hunted down, and all were either killed or captured.

An army of five full regiments and two batteries, with all necessary supplies and equipment, had been assembled at Fort Riley in Kansas, in April, 1862, to march to the relief of New Mexico. On hearing of the defeat of the Confederates at La Gloriéta, and of their retreat from Santa Fé and probable speedy withdrawal from New Mexico, the order for this force to advance was countermanded by the war department, and a large part of it was sent at once to strengthen the Union movements in Tennessee.   Thus was saved, in this instance alone, to the government at Washington, an expenditure of money estimated in a report to the quartermaster-general of the United States army, at ten millions of dollars, and the services of regiments which were sorely needed elsewhere.

These Federal military operations in the Southwest were seriously embarrassed by the difficulties and delays in the transmission of communications to and from Washington, and by the neglect, whether intentional or not, of the authorities at Washington. Concerning the latter, Jerome C. Smiley, in his *History of Denver* (1901), quotes (page 386) the following from the testimony of Colonel Benjamin S. Roberts, of Colonel Canby's command, before the congressional committee on the conduct of the war, on July 15, 1862:

"It appears to me to be the determination of General Thomas [Lorenzo Thomas, then adjutant-general of the United States army] not to acknowledge the services of the officers who saved the Territory of New Mexico; and the utter neglect of the Adjutant-General's department for the last year to communicate in any way with the commanding officer of the Department of New Mexico, or to answer his urgent appeals for reinforcements, for money and for other supplies, in connection with his repudiation of the services of all the army there, convinces me that he is not gratified at their loyalty and their success in saving that Territory to the Union."

CONCLUSION.

While the work of the Colorado Volunteers in utterly crushing the vaulting ambitions and far-reaching expectations with which the Confederates had entered New Mexico had been sharp, short and decisive, the misfortunes of war had fallen heavily upon them. On preceding pages the totals of Union losses in killed and in wounded from the beginning of the campaign, according to the several but differing reports of various officers, have been given; and the imperfections and incompleteness of the Civil War records in the department of the adjutant-general of Colorado have been mentioned. The deficiencies of the latter became more and more apparent as the task of gathering the names of Colorado soldiers who were either killed or wounded in that campaign proceeded. The war department, at Washington, was asked to assist in this, but in reply said that "owing to the limited clerical force allowed by law and the pressure of important current work, the Department can not undertake to compile and furnish lists showing the names of the killed and wounded in the engagements referred to." Therefore, the resources at hand in Denver had to be depended on entirely. The following lists of killed and wounded, by name and company, were compiled, partly from the records in the Colorado adjutant-general's department, and partly from other reports, from files of the Denver newspapers of 1862, and from Hollister's pamphlet—from which some quotations have been made on other pages. In those of the killed the names of several men whose wounds directly caused their death, and with one exception within a short time, are included. While the lists are as complete as the most careful search among available sources of information could make them, it is not improbable that they contain some inaccuracies, and that a few names (beside those of Captain Dodd's unknown wounded at Valverdé and of those who may have been wounded at Péralta, as noted) which should be in them are missing.

(143)

AT VALVERDÉ.

CAPTAIN DODD'S INDEPENDENT COMPANY.

Colonel Canby, in his final report of the battle of Valverdé, stated that two men of this company were killed, and twenty-eight wounded. The records in the Colorado adjutant-general's department show that two more died from wounds within a day or two, and that seven (those named below) were "discharged for disability from wounds received at Valverdé," but they contain no account of the other wounded, who, it is to be presumed, recovered and continued in the service.

KILLED.

Brown, Hugh.
McKee, John.
West, Nelson A.
Woodward, Harrison B.

WOUNDED.

Bridgman, Frederick W.,
Duffy, Patrick H.,
Finch, Francis L.,
Newman, James L.,
Pampaugh, Frank,
Talbot, Asa,
Young, John W.,

and, according to Colonel Canby, nineteen more, who could not be identified for this work.

AT LA GLORIÉTA.

In the following list of the killed and wounded in the two engagements in La Gloriéta pass, the date of the first fight follows the names of those who could be identified as having suffered in that encounter:

KILLED.

Anderson, Christopher—Company D.
Baker, Lieutenant John—Company I.
Barton, Charles—Company D.

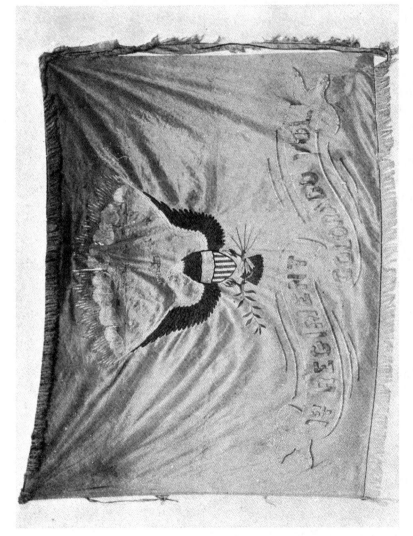

Regimental Standard of the First Regiment, Colorado Volunteers.

(From a photograph of the flag, which is now in the War-relic Department of the Headquarters of the Grand Army of the Republic, Department of Colorado and Wyoming, in the Capitol at Denver.)

Billard, Frank—Company C.

Bird, Samuel—Company I.

Boon, Hopkins M.—Company C.

Boyle, Michael E.—Company D.

Butler, Christian—Company G.

Chambers, Lieutenant Clark—Company C.

Creitz, Charles—Company D.

Davis, Alfred—Company D.

Denny, Alfred J.—Company D.

Dutro, Martin—Company F.   (March 26th.)

Edwards, William G.—Company D.   (March 26th.)

Elliott, John B.—Company D.

Fenner, Charles—Company D.

Freres, John—Company I.

Garwish, John—Company I.

Griffin, John M.—Ford's Independent Company.

Hanley, Henry C.—Company K.

Hatshkiss, Jasper—Company I.

Hirshhausen, Henry—Company I.

Hittig, Gottlieb—Company I.

Honeywell, Lyman—Company I.

Hurst, Sergeant William H.—Company I.

Hutson, Jarett—Company G.

James, William—Company D.

Johnson, Armand—Company I.

Johnson, Jude W.—Company F.   (March 26th.)

Jones, Moses—Company K.

Kreider, John—Company I.

Lovelace, Harmon—Company G.

Marshall, Lieutenant William F.—Company F.   (March 26th.)

Mattaush, Ignatz—Company I.

McMillan, John J.—Company D.

Peters, Amos R.—Company C.

Pomps, Andrew—Company C.

Renderly, John—Company I.

Rufer, Frederick—Company I.

Schuler, Adam—Company D.
Seeley, J. G.—Company D.
Seymour, O. C.—Company G.
Shepherd, John E.—Company D.
Slawson, Ilzatus—Company D.
Smith, Jacob—Company C.
Stewart, John H.—Company I.
Stone, Matthew—Company D.
Thompson, George—Company F. (March 26th.)

WOUNDED.

Backus, Henry—Company I.
Baker, Benjamin—Company D.
Baldwin, William—Company C.
Bartlett, August—Company I.
Bowmand, William—Company I.
Brass, Frank—Company I.
Bristol, Charles H.—Company F.   (March 26th.)
Clisbee, William S.—Company G.
Cook, Captain Samuel H.—Company F.   (March 26th.)
Cudmore, William—Company I.
Davis, John W.—Company D.
Donaldson, James—Company K.
Downing, Josiah D.—Company D.
Doyle, James—Company I.
Eichbaum, William F.—Company K.
Elliott, William—Company D.
Fall, George W.—Company D.
Ferris, Benjamin F.—Company F.
Fihlhauser, John C.—Company C.
Fleming, John F.—Company D.
Flinn, Joseph—Company D.
Foote, Talmadge O.—Company D.
Ford, William G.—Company G.
Freeman, O. I.—Company F.
Gerard, Austin—Company I.
Gould, E. C.—Company F.

Banner of the Veteran Battalion of the First
Colorado Regiment, After the Organization
Was Transferred to the Cavalry Arm.

(From a photograph of the banner, which is
now in the War-relic Department of the
Headquarters of the Grand Army of the Republic, Department of Colorado and Wyoming, in the Capitol at Denver.)

The figure of a lamb, with the word "Pet"
above it, on the banner, was adopted as a battalion emblem in memory of the term, "Pet
Lambs," applied to the regiment by the soldiers of General Sibley's army up to the day
of the second battle in La Glorieta Pass.

Grealich, James—Company K.

Griffin, Edwin B.—Company D.

Hall, William F.—Company F.   (March 26th.)

Hawes, Thomas J.—Company D.

Henry, John—Company I.

Hicks, Charles D.—Company D.

Iler, William—Company D.

Johnson, Edward F.—Company G.

Johnson, Henry—Company I.

Johnson, Peter—Company D.

Keegan, Patrick—Company D.

Keel, Jesse F.—Company F.   (March 26th.)

Kemball, Henry—Company I.

Kohler, John—Company D.

Logan, C. W.—Company F.   (March 26th.)

Laughlin, Matthew—Company D.

McDonald, Angus—Company K.

Meggers, Frederick—Company I.

Muxlow, William—Company G.

Newcomer, John—Company D.

Niedhardt, George—Company I.

Oleson, Ole—Company I.

Oren, H. H.—Company K.

Osborne, Edward W.—Company G.

Owens, George—Company D.

Patterson, M. A.—Company F.   (March 26th.)

Pierce, Isaac N.—Company C.

Pratt, A. B.—Company F.   (March 26th.)

Prickett, Edward—Company D.

Rail, Philip—Company C.

Ritter, Simon—Company A.

Schneider, John T.—Company C.

Smith, John—Company I.

Tosh, Joseph W.—Company C.

Wales, Thomas H.—Company K.

Ward, Peter—Company I.

Wilbur, Charles E.—Company D.
Wilcox, Willis—Company C.
Yates, Richard—Company C.

AT PÉRALTA.

Colonel Canby's report of the affair at Péralta says his loss there was "one killed and three wounded." Other records, principally those of the Colorado adjutant-general's department, mention four deaths among the Colorado Volunteers from that engagement, but contain nothing as to non-fatal wounds.

KILLED.

Hawley, J. H.—Company F.
Long, Joseph—Company C.
Thompson, George—Ford's Independent Company.
Wilson, Martin—Company C.

In the foregoing lists of the dead we have the names of fifty-six men, and in those of the wounded the names of seventy-two. Adding to the latter the nineteen unknown wounded at Valverdé raises the number of wounded to ninety-one, making the total casualties of the Colorado Volunteers, during the campaign, of less than three months' time, 147. Of this total the dead at La Gloriéta numbered forty-eight, and the wounded sixty-five; in all, 113. There was nearly a score of men who were merely brushed or scratched at La Gloriéta, and did not go off duty or have any hospital record, and therefore are not included in this total. Except one man, of Ford's Independent Company, killed, and one of Company A, First Colorado, wounded, these La Gloriéta losses were borne by Companies C, D, F, G, I and K of the regiment. Company A, as the reader has seen, was in the first fight there, but it escaped loss; and in the second fight Ford's company and Companies A, B, E and H were in Chivington's division, that destroyed the Confederate encampment and wagon train at Johnson's ranch, in which enterprise only one man, a member of Company A, was injured.

The brunt of the La Gloriéta losses fell upon Company D, Captain Downing, and Company I, Captain Mailie. Captain Downing had sixteen men killed and twenty wounded; the extraordinary total of thirty-six—the heaviest casualties sustained by any company organization engaged in the campaign. Captain Mailie's were nearly as many—fifteen killed and fifteen wounded. In each of these companies there were several men touched skin deep, but who are not counted here.

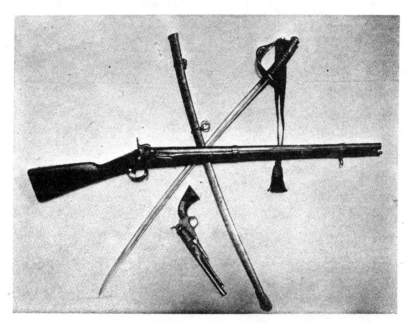

Types of Arms Used by the Colorado Volunteers in the New Mexico Campaign.
(From a photograph of weapons in the varied collection in the War-relic Department of the Headquarters of the Grand Army of the Republic, Department of Colorado and Wyoming, in the Capitol at Denver.)

The reader is reminded that the casualties enumerated above are only those which occurred among the Colorado Volunteers. Of those of the several small detachments of other troops that fought in the Apache cañon and at Pigeon's ranch no reports were available. Such losses as those in the two conflicts that constituted the battle of La Gloriéta, occurring proportionately in a struggle between two of the immense armies in the East, would have appalled the country—North and South. While the Union casualty list is long, that of the Confederates probably was twice its length, and possibly even more.

Probably some Colorado Volunteers were wounded in the final fight with Sibley's forces at Péralta, and survived their injuries, but no record of them could be found.

The number of deaths from disease among the Colorado troops, from the time they were mustered into the service until the defeat and retreat of General Sibley's army, was remarkably small, not exceeding eight or ten, a fact in which was reflected the excellent physical character of the men. In July, 1862, three were drowned in the Rio Grandé—Sergeant John Callery of Company C, First Colorado, on the 5th, at Fort Craig; Frank Quinn, of Ford's Independent Company, on the 6th, at Fort Craig, and Harvey A. Murphy, of Company A, First Colorado, on the 22d, at Valverdé.

Captain Edward W. Wynkoop.
(From a war-time photograph in the State Historical and Natural History Society's collection.)
Captain Wynkoop was promoted Major of the First Colorado Regiment in April, 1862, for distinguished services.

In the spring of 1862, after the Péralta fight with General Sibley's decimated and retreating command, there were several resignations and various promotions among the company officers of the First Colorado. Chivington having become colonel of the regiment, Captain Wynkoop, of Company A, was promoted major to succeed him. At that time, also, Lieutenant Roath, of Company D, and Lieutenant Sanford, of Company E, resigned; and at the close of May Captain Sopris and Lieutenant Cobb, of Company C, and in June Captain Mailie, of Company I, likewise retired. Lieutenant Chambers, of Company C, who had been so badly wounded at La Gloriéta, and who died of his injuries in the following March, was promoted

captain, but only to be discharged, on account of disability, in November of that year. Following these advancements and resignations, and to fill one or two other vacancies, there were many promotions in regular order, and several transfers from one company
to another. Lieutenants moved a step higher, and sergeants became
lieutenants. But I shall leave the particulars of these promotions
to some one who may undertake the worthy task of writing in full
the history of all of Colorado's volunteer military organizations in
the War for the Union.

On July 4th Colonel Chivington was relieved of the command of
Fort Craig and of the Southern District by Colonel Howe, of the
Third United States Cavalry. He then reported in person to
Colonel Canby at Santa Fé, and procured an order to move the
First Colorado to Fort Union, and also obtained leave of absence
to proceed to Washington for the purpose of seeking to have his
regiment made a cavalry organization and transferred to the Army
of the Potomac. Of the outcome of Colonel Chivington's mission
to the national capital, and of the further services of the regiment
after the close of the campaign in New Mexico, General Frank
Hall, in his *History of Colorado* (1889), says (volume I, page 286
and page 287):

"He failed to obtain the transfer to the Army of the Potomac,
but by dint of great perseverance he did obtain an order of transfer
to the cavalry arm, and for the relief of his regiment from further
service in New Mexico; also for its return to Colorado for service
there, where it arrived in detachments about the first of January,
1863, and was mounted, and continued in the service in Colorado
and the adjacent territories during the remainder of the war. The
horses and horse equipments and change of arms, etc., were received
and the regiment was mounted soon after its arrival in the territory
of Colorado, and was then distributed at the various posts in that
territory, and at several camps established, to render it more effective in holding in check the Indians who had become hostile. And
it may be observed here that the Indian outbreak, from New Ulm,
Minnesota to the Arkansas river, was as veritable a part of the Rebellion as the revolt of the whites in any part of the Southern
states. * * *."

"After New Mexico had been liberated there were no further
glories, no more battlefields, for the First Colorado Though some

of its detached companies rendered efficient service in the Indian wars which ensued, as a whole its record ended with the flight of Sibley. * * * "

Such a regiment as the First Colorado had proved itself to be, inspired by such a leader as Chivington had proved himself to be, certainly would have still further highly distinguished itself had its field of action been widened by the transfer of the organization to the Army of the Potomac, for which Chivington had appealed, but which, to his great disappointment, and to that of his men, also, was denied.

Captain Scott J. Anthony.
(From a war-time photograph loaned by Mr. Samuel C. Dorsey, of Denver.)
Captain Anthony was promoted Major of the First Colorado Regiment when it was made a cavalry organization.

The other two organizations of Colorado Volunteers which participated in the New Mexico campaign —the independent companies of Captains Ford and Dodd—remained in that territory until well into the next year, doing duty at Fort Craig, Santa Fé and Fort Union. At the time when General Sibley began his retreat down the Rio Grandé valley, Dodd's company was still a part of Colonel Canby's immediate command, and Ford's went into the valley with the First Colorado regiment to join Canby, with whose army it proceeded to Fort Craig. Late in the spring of 1863 the two companies returned to Colorado to take their places in the Second regiment of Colorado Volunteer Infantry, for which they were originally intended, but which had been delayed in coming into existence. Ford's became Company A and Dodd's Company B, a reversal of their designations when mustered into the service in December, 1861. Captain Dodd was promoted lieutenant-colonel of the regiment and Captain Ford major. Later, Colonel Jesse H. Leavenworth having been removed, Dodd was promoted colonel. In the winter of 1863-4 the Second was consolidated with the incomplete Third regiment of Colorado Volunteer Infantry, the new organization being converted into the Second regiment of Colorado Volunteer Cavalry, of which Major Ford, who eventually attained the rank of brigadier-general, was promoted colonel, with Dodd as lieutenant-colonel.

The people of New Mexico, through their legislature, erected in the plaza at Santa Fé, within three years after the close of the Civil War, a plain and unpretending soldiers' monument, having four marble tablets, on two of which are appropriate inscriptions that honor the soldiers of the Federal army who fell in the engagements with the Confederates in the territory. These several inscriptions read as follows:

"Erected by the People of New Mexico, through their Legislatures of 1866, '7, '8. May the Union be Perpetuated."
"To the Heroes who have Fallen in the Various Battles with Savage Indians in the Territory of New Mexico."
"To the Heroes of the Federal Army who fell at the Battle of Valverdé, fought with the Rebels, February 21, 1862."
"To the Heroes of the Federal Army who fell at the Battles in Cañon del Apache and Pigeon's Rancho (La Gloriéta), fought with the Rebels, March 28, 1862; and to those who fell at the Battle fought with the Rebels at Péralto, April 15, 1862."

Laying the corner stone of this monument was made the occasion of a rather elaborate and impressive ceremony, in which the governor of Colorado territory, "the soldiers of Colorado Regiments," and "the people of the Territory of Colorado generally," were invited to participate, as witness the following communication received by Governor A. C. Hunt:

"Santa Fe, New Mexico, October 1, 1867.
"Governor:
"The corner stone of the monument to be erected in honor of the dead heroes of the battlefields of 'Valverdé,' 'Apache Cañon' and 'Pigeon's Ranch' (La Gloriéta), in the Plaza of Santa Fé, our Capital, pursuant to the wish of the people of this Territory, as expressed through the Governor and the Legislative Assembly, will be laid with appropriate ceremonies on Thursday, the twenty-fourth day of the present month.

Catholic Church.   Governor's Palace.   Parogula.   Catholic Church.

VIEW of SANTA FE.

Protestant Church.   Unfinished Capitol.   **View of Santa Fe in the Civil War Period.**   Pavilion.   Military Hospital.

(From a photograph—loaned by Mr. Max. Frost, of Santa Fe—of a painting by Anthony Kellner, a private soldier of the Fifth Regiment United States Infantry.)

"As Colorado mourns the loss of many of her brave sons, who, on the battlefields of this Territory, gave their lives in defense of the Constitution and the Union, it is hoped that your Territory will be represented on the occasion.

"In behalf, therefore, of the grateful people of New Mexico, we extend to you, and through you to the soldiers of Colorado Regiments, and to the people of Colorado Territory generally, an invitation to be present and participate in the ceremonies of the occasion.

"We are, Governor,

"With much respect, your most ob't serv'ts,

"H. H. HEATH,

"Secretary of the Territory of New Mexico.

"JOHN P. SLOUGH,

"Chief Justice of the Territory of New Mexico.

"FELIPE DELGADO,

"Treasurer Monument Association.

"To the Governor of Colorado Territory, Golden City, C. T."

Upon receipt of this invitation a call was issued for a public meeting, at Denver City, of the soldiers of Colorado, to appoint a committee to attend and take part in the ceremonies of laying the corner stone of the Santa Fé monument. The meeting appointed the following named gentlemen to constitute this committee: Former Governor John Evans, D. Washington Griffey and Charles G. Chever. This committee went to Santa Fé at the appointed time and received a warm welcome. Upon its return its members made the following public report:

"Denver, November 3, 1867.

"To the Soldiers of Colorado:

"Gentlemen: In pursuance of your request, we were present at the ceremonies of laying the corner stone of the monument being erected by the Territory of New Mexico in memory of the patriotic dead who fell on her battlefields.

"It was especially gratifying to your committee, as it must be to you, to witness this public work of respect to your fallen comrades; and the hospitality of the people of New Mexico, extended to your committee, shows how fully they appreciated those we represented. As a mark of the gratitude felt by the people of that Territory for the valiant services rendered them in the hour of their peril, they are worthy of your highest appreciation. But especially should their course, in erecting this monument to the memory of those who fell in the cause of freedom and our common country, commend their patriotism and loyalty to our warmest approbation and most hearty thanks.

Soldier's Monument in the Plaza at Santa Fe.
(From a photograph in the State Historical and Natural History Society's collection.)

"Herewith please find a copy of the proceedings of the ceremony of laying the corner stone, and believe us,

"Very respectfully,

"Your obedient servants,

"JOHN EVANS.

"D. WASHINGTON GRIFFEY.

"CHARLES G. CHEVER."

The corner stone was laid under the auspices of the Order of Free and Accepted Masons, and with the customary ceremonies of that organization. A large number and variety of documents and other things were deposited in it, among which was a parchment bearing the names of all of the Union officers who fought in the battles of Valverdé, La Gloriéta and Péralta. It was the intention of the Monument Association also to deposit in the stone a complete list of the names of the dead to whom the memorial was raised, but these could not be obtained in time. The association then comforted itself with the belief that they could be collected later, and "deposited in another part of the monument, with suitable reference."

The time will surely come when some worthy memorial, either a towering shaft or a public edifice, will be raised and dedicated by the people of Colorado, in their capital city, to their hardy and intrepid volunteers who fought for the preservation of the Union; and especially to those who constituted their First regiment, whose staunch patriotism and willing sacrifices were exhibited, without any reserve, in aiding so effectively to preserve a vast territory in the West and in the Southwest to the Union, and whose riddled and torn battle flag is still cherished as a sacred emblem.

INDEX

The Battle of
GLORIETA PASS
THE COLORADO VOLUNTEERS
IN THE CIVIL WAR
March 26, 27, 28, 1862

William C. Whitford

With a factual analysis of
the military strategy of both sides,
illustrated with explanatory maps
compiled and drawn by
Burt Schmitz of Cupertino, California

APPENDIX

A RIO GRANDE CLASSIC
First Published in 1906

LIBRARY OF CONGRESS CARD CATALOG
74-150964

ISBN 0-87380-171-7

1994

The Rio Grande Press, Inc.

GLORIETA, NEW MEXICO · 87535

COMMENTARY

Having brought my enthusiasm for the Civil War with me from Indiana in the mid-fifties and only recently arrived in Denver, I soon found myself elected to the Civil War Round Table of Colorado and shortly, I served a term as secretary in 1957. I had heard vague rumors that there had been a big Civil War battle somewhere in the west involving Colorado miners. But like so many people from the east, mostly through the sin of omission, I, too, had taken for granted the idea that any Civil War action west of the Mississippi was most probably a myth.

Then I noted yet another reference to this battle in the *Denver Post.* That did it! Who else to call but the Colorado State Historical Society! Not only did these fine people confirm it, they even had a few copies remaining of a book somebody named Whitford had written in 1906, that told all about the battles and the whole New Mexico campaign! And that unknown voice on the phone told me: " . . . the book originally sold for $1.00, and we don't have any reason to change it."

So armed with my collector's edition book, enthusiasm, and a lunch, I started out for the wilds of Santa Fe 500 miles away. I found three old men, now dead, who had actually talked with veterans of the battle. With the guidance of these local sources and the photographs in Whitford, I found the battle site!

Now, thirty-four years later, I am in awe that my research has come full circle and honored that The Rio Grande Press has asked my permission—readily granted—to include these maps and analyses in this new, enlarged and amplified edition of *The Battle of Glorieta Pass; The Colorado Volunteers in the Civil War,* by William C. Whitford, first published in 1906.

Over the years, my love affair with the history of the westernmost battle of the Civil War has led me to read many of the accounts and reminiscences by veterans and other researchers, accounts that have and will continue to surface. These have all expanded my knowledge and understanding of the battle. But in the end, I have always come back to the first-hand accounts of the participants as reported in the *Official Records of the Civil War, Operations in Texas, New Mexico and Arizona* (Ch. XXI, pages 530 to 545) and the broader account researched and written by Dr. Whitford.

In the text supporting the maps that follow, for simplicity, all direct quotes are from either the Official Records or from Whitford. This does not denigrate the other sources. Perhaps the reader will find information that refines, expands on, or even changes some of the material in theses texts or my maps. History has never been an absolute, even 100 hours after an event—let alone over 100 years.

Burt Schmitz

Cupertino, California
June 1991

EIGHT DETAILED AND ANNOTATED MAPS

COMMENTARY

If military historians have a bane, it is certainly the dearth of maps that authors, for no good reason, customarily omit from their narratives. William C. Whitford's classic on the 1862 New Mexico Campaign, *The Battle of Glorieta Pass; The Colorado Volunteers in the Civil War,* fits this mold. While it contains excellent graphic documentation of the battlefield, portraits or photographs of key participants, and even includes maps of the battle of Valverde and the region, it does not contain a single map of the Battle of Glorieta Pass. Burt Schmitz, a long-time student of the conflict there, has changed all of that.

Mr. Schmitz has produced eight detailed and annotated maps of the Glorieta action of March 26-28, 1862, that are included in this new edition by The Rio Grande Press of Glorieta itself. These maps are certain to enhance and satisfy the most consummate battle buff's demand for precise information on battlefield terrain and troop movements. The author's maps are the product of more than 30 years of research and refinement. Although the maps are the interpretations of the author, they have at their foundation the historical analysis of William C. Whitford; thus, it can be said that the maps are an extension of Whitford's study. They are an invaluable resource addition which contributes significantly to the understanding and appreciation of the human events that transpired on the slopes of Glorieta Pass.

Neil C. Mangum

Regional Historian,
National Park Service, Southwest Region,
Santa Fe, New Mexico

4

GLORIETA, APACHE CANYON
26 MARCH 1862
AFTERNOON: 2:00 PM

ORDER OF BATTLE (more or less):

FEDERAL:

Maj. CHIVINGTON.

    Regular Army;
        3rd Cavalry,
            Capt. HOWLAND, Lt. WALL, Lt. FALVEY
            Co. C, 28 men.
            Co. D, 6 men.
            Co. __, 6 men.
            Co. K, 10 men.
        3rd Cavalry,
            Capt. WALKER, Lt. BANKS
            Co. E, 50 men.
        1st Cavalry,
            Capt. LORD, Lt. BERNARD
            Co's. D, G, 50 men.

    1st Regt. Colo. Inf. Vol.:
        Capt. WYNKOOP; Co. A, 60 men.
        Capt. DOWNING; Co. D, 60 men.
        Capt. ANTHONY; Co. E, 60 men.
        Capt. COOK; Co. F, (Mounted Infantry), 88 men. (Note: Maj. CHIVINGTON
            in his report in O.R. also identified these as "Co. F, First
            Regiment Cavalry Colorado Volunteers." The identification as
            cavalry appears on both maps A and B.)

    Total = 418 men.

CONFEDERATE:

    Maj. PYRON:
        Estimated to have had 600 men at Canyoncito, although how many of
        these men were ahead in the Apache Canyon advance appears to be
        undetermined. Maj. PYRON sent an urgent message to Lt. Col. SCURRY
        in late afternoon describing an engagement with "a greatly superior
        force of the enemy."

        The Confederate losses were 7 officers wounded; 32 men killed, 43
        wounded, and 71 taken prisoner = 146 total loss.

APACHE CANYON, UPPER BATTLEFIELD
AFTERNOON: 2:30 PM
(APACHE CANYON, MAP A)

As the Federal advance guard entered Apache Canyon, 2 Confederate Lts. and

30 men were captured at a turn in the road and narrow gulch on the descent. The Federal main force under CHIVINGTON was 3/4 mile back in the pass on the Santa Fe Trail *(nearing the summit at Interstate I-25)*. The Federals descended the Santa Fe Trail into the flat of the upper battlefield and immediately took cover behind the ridge to shelter from the Confederate battery of 2 howitzers and the mounted infantry guard. Capt. HOWLAND with the US Cavalry and Capt. COOK with the Colorado mounted infantry, Co. F, were sent to the rear to charge the artillery if it was seen to be in retreat.

Co. A, WYNKOOP, Co. E, ANTHONY, and Capt. WALKER with the dismounted cavalry were sent as skirmishers to the left among the trees on the mountainside. Co. D, Capt. DOWNING were sent to skirmish on the mountainside on the right. Parties of volunteers and regulars assembled behind the ridge to form the Federal center. The Confederate troops were driven in on their howitzers, and preparations were made by the Confederates to retreat back down the canyon. Capt. HOWLAND failed to follow his orders to charge the retreating Confederates.

APACHE CANYON, LOWER BATTLEFIELD
FIRST POSITION
AFTERNOON: 3:30 PM
(APACHE CANYON, MAP A)

The Confederates retreated down the canyon, crossed the log bridge, then dumped it into the arroyo. They set up the battery on a small rise, and placed their supports on the mountainsides, "completely covering" both sides of the Canyon. CHIVINGTON's Federal plan of attack remained essentially the same as before; Co. D, DOWNING, augmented by HOWLAND's now dismounted Cavalry on the right; Co. A, WYNKOOP, Co. E, ANTHONY, and WALKER with dismounted Cavalry on the left. The Colorado mounted infantry, Co. F, under Capt. COOK was now assigned the responsibility to charge if the Confederate battery was seen to be in retreat.

APACHE CANYON, LOWER BATTLEFIELD
SECOND POSITION
AFTERNOON: 4:30 PM to SUNDOWN
(APACHE CANYON, MAP B)

After one hour, with DOWNING nearly flanking the Confederate left, the Confederate supports were driven in and the artillery routed. At this, the mounted infantry, Co. F, Capt. COOK, with some 100 mounted troops (per Whitford, 103; per Chivington, 88 of Co. F), drove on and leaped the open arroyo at the bridge, then charged 3 times through the Confederate troops and back. The Confederates who hadn't escaped back down the Santa Fe Trail to Canyoncito were driven across the arroyo and up a side canyon by DOWNING and the dismounted Cavalry, Co. C, 3rd Cavalry, Lt. BERNARD, where they were taken prisoner.

NOTE: Line 3 text in italic letters changed June, 1994.

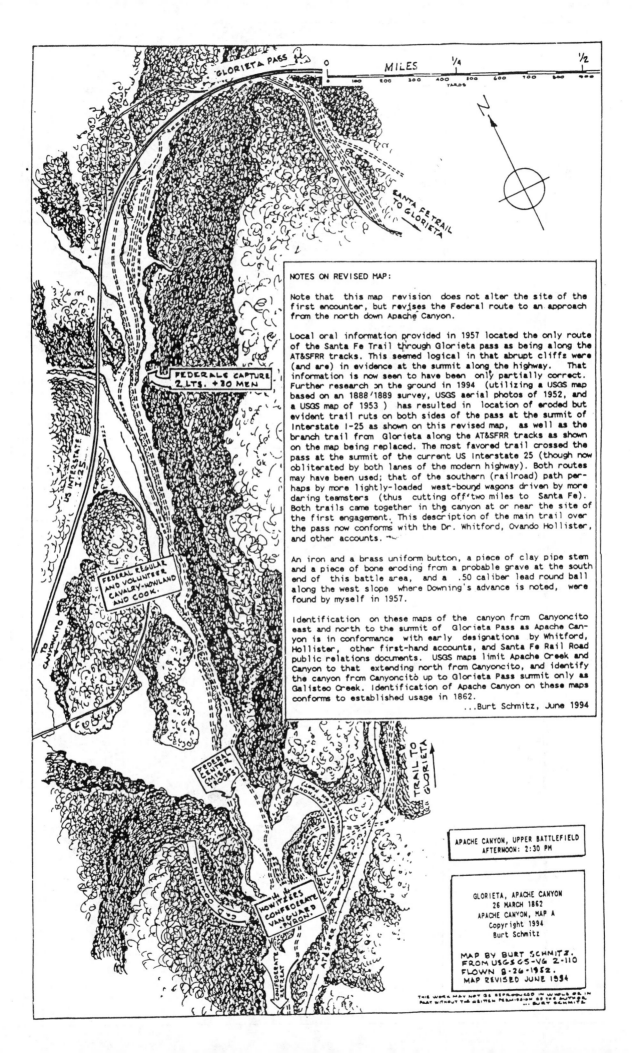

MILES

YARDS

GLORIETA PASS

SANTA FE TRAIL
TO GLORIETA

N

FEDERALS CAPTURE
2 LTS. + 30 MEN

US INTERSTATE I-25

FEDERAL REGULAR
AND VOLUNTEER
CAVALRY-HOWLAND
AND COOK.

TO CANYONCITO

FEDERAL
CENTER
(MISC. TROOPS)

TRAIL TO GLORIETA

HOWITZERS
CONFEDERATE
VANGUARD
PYRON.

CONFEDERATE

AT&SFRR

NOTES ON REVISED MAP:

Note that this map revision does not alter the site of the first encounter, but revises the Federal route to an approach from the north down Apache Canyon.

Local oral information provided in 1957 located the only route of the Santa Fe Trail through Glorieta pass as being along the AT&SFRR tracks. This seemed logical in that abrupt cliffs were (and are) in evidence at the summit along the highway. That information is now seen to have been only partially correct. Further research on the ground in 1994 (utilizing a USGS map based on an 1888′1889 survey, USGS aerial photos of 1952, and a USGS map of 1953) has resulted in location of eroded but evident trail ruts on both sides of the pass at the summit of Interstate I-25 as shown on this revised map, as well as the branch trail from Glorieta along the AT&SFRR tracks as shown on the map being replaced. The most favored trail crossed the pass at the summit of the current US Interstate 25 (though now obliterated by both lanes of the modern highway). Both routes may have been used; that of the southern (railroad) path perhaps by more lightly-loaded west-bound wagons driven by more daring teamsters (thus cutting off two miles to Santa Fe). Both trails came together in the canyon at or near the site of the first engagement. This description of the main trail over the pass now conforms with the Dr. Whitford, Ovando Hollister, and other accounts.

An iron and a brass uniform button, a piece of clay pipe stem and a piece of bone eroding from a probable grave at the south end of this battle area, and a .50 caliber lead round ball along the west slope where Downing's advance is noted, were found by myself in 1957.

Identification on these maps of the canyon from Canyoncito east and north to the summit of Glorieta Pass as Apache Canyon is in conformance with early designations by Whitford, Hollister, other first-hand accounts, and Santa Fe Rail Road public relations documents. USGS maps limit Apache Creek and Canyon to that extending north from Canyoncito, and identify the canyon from Canyoncito up to Glorieta Pass summit only as Galisteo Creek. Identification of Apache Canyon on these maps conforms to established usage in 1862.

...Burt Schmitz, June 1994

APACHE CANYON, UPPER BATTLEFIELD
AFTERNOON: 2:30 PM

GLORIETA, APACHE CANYON
26 MARCH 1862
APACHE CANYON, MAP A
Copyright 1994
Burt Schmitz

MAP BY BURT SCHMITZ.
FROM USGS GS-VG 2-110
FLOWN 8-26-1952.
MAP REVISED JUNE 1994

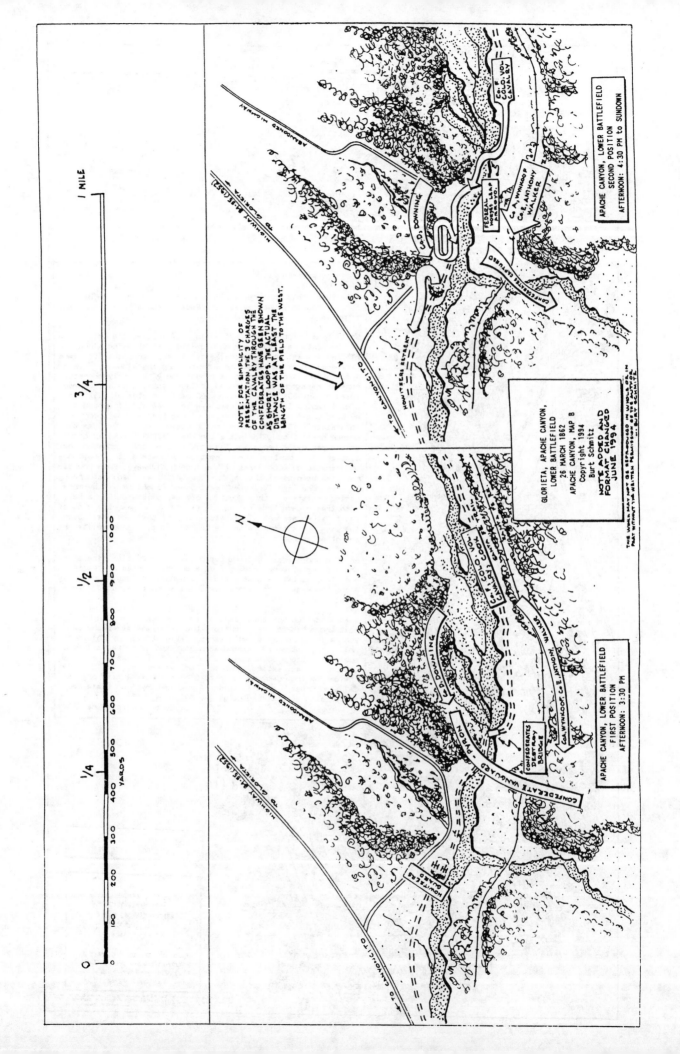

GLORIETA, APACHE CANYON,
LOWER BATTLEFIELD
26 MARCH 1862
APACHE CANYON, MAP B
Copyright 1994
Burt Schmitz
NOTE ADDED AND
FORMAT CHANGED
JUNE 1994

THIS WORK MAY NOT BE REPRODUCED IN WHOLE OR IN
PART WITHOUT THE WRITTEN PERMISSION OF THE AUTHOR,
BURT SCHMITZ

NOTE: FOR SIMPLICITY OF
PRESENTATION THE 3 CHARGES
OF THE CAVALRY THROUGH THE
CONFEDERATES HAVE BEEN SHOWN
AS SHORT LOOPS. THE ACTUAL
DISTANCE WAS AT LEAST THE
LENGTH OF THE FIELD TO THE WEST.

APACHE CANYON, LOWER BATTLEFIELD
SECOND POSITION
AFTERNOON: 4:30 PM to SUNDOWN

APACHE CANYON, LOWER BATTLEFIELD
FIRST POSITION
AFTERNOON: 3:30 PM

GLORIETA, PIGEON'S RANCH
28 MARCH 1862
FIRST POSITION
MORNING: 10:00-11:00 AM
(MAP No. 1)

ORDER OF BATTLE (more or less):

FEDERAL:

Col. SLOUGH.
   First Colorado Volunteers; 916.
   Fifth Infantry, Capt. LEWIS and Fourth New Mexico Volunteers, Capt. FORD;
191.
   First and Third Cavalry, Capt. HOWLAND; 150.

   Lt. Col. TAPPAN's command at Pigeon's.
      Infantry: First Colorado Vounteer Co. C, Capt. SOPRIS; Co. D, Capt.
   DOWNING; Co. G, Capt. WILDER; Co. I, Capt. MAILIE (German's, Lt.
   KERBER); Co. K, Capt. ROBBINS.

      Artillery: Capt. RITTER, Lt MCGRATH, Lt. UNDERHILL, 4 gun battery;
   two 12 pounders, two 6 pounders, 50 men. (Also recorded, 53 men.)
   Lt. CLAFLIN, four 12 pound mountain howitzers, 32 men.

Total; 1342. (Less 430 detached under CHIVINGTON) = 912 available at
      Pigeon's Ranch.

CONFEDERATE:

Lt. Col. SCURRY.
      Maj. RAGUET
      Maj. SHROPSHIRE
      Maj. PYRON

      Fourth Regiment (portions of 9 companies); Capt's. HAMPTON, LESUEUR,
FOARD, CROSSON, GIESECKE, ALEXANDER, BUCKHOLTS, ODELL, and Co. B, Lt. HOLLAND
(Capt. SCARBOROUGH ill). Seventh Regiment (4 companies); Capt's. HOFFMAN,
GARDNER, WIGGINS, ADAIR. Fifth Regiment (4 companies); Capt's. SHANNON,
RAGSDALE, and Lts. OAKES and SCOTT. Artillery; Lt. BRADFORD, 3 pieces; Capt.
PHILLIPS' Independent Volunteers Company. (After BRADFORD was wounded at the
1st position, the Confederate artillery withdrew. SCURRY then ordered 2 pieces
to return forward under Pvt. KIRK of PHILLIPS' and Sgt. PATRICK, Artillery,
who continued the gunnery for the Confederates.)

Total = 600 ("fit for duty" per SCURRY).
      ...a total of about 1,100 men." Whitford, page 99.

SHROPSHIRE, RAGUET, Capt. BUCKHOLTS, Lt. MILLS killed later during the day's
action.

      NOTE: Text in italic letters added June, 1994.

GLORIETA, FIRST POSITION, OPENING
MORNING: 10:00-11:00 AM

Note: A variety of times for the start and duration of this clash have been reported. SLOUGH, 10:30 (O.R. 534). SCURRY, 11:00 UNTIL 5:30. TAPPAN, 1/2 hour in this first position (O.R. 536).

The terrain has been described as "The fighting was all done in THICK COVERS OF CEDARS..." per SLOUGH, and "Glorieta, situated in a deep, narrow, thickly wooded canyon," per TAPPAN (O.R. 536).

GENERAL:

Col. SLOUGH's army units arrived at Pigeon's Ranch over a period of 1 1/2 hours, from 8:30 AM (though SLOUGH says in his report 9:00) to 10:00 AM (or, again per SLOUGH 10:30); HOWLAND's Cavalry was in the advance (though his command of the cavalry during this battle is conspicuous by its absence after his failure to charge at Apache Canyon on the 26th). The supply train of 100 plus wagon's and the guard in the rear took position down the Santa Fe Trail in the flat (east) behind Pigeon's Ranch. By this time most of the body of Federal troops had arrived at Pigeon's.
(WALKER states in O.R. he had been there for 1 1/2 hours, i.e., 8:30 AM. However, if SLOUGH left Kowalski's at 9:00 AM to arrive at Pigeon's at 10:30, WALKER's reported time would have been more nearly 9:00 AM, and also the first Confederates on the Santa Fe Trail about 1/2 mile west.)

Capt. CHAPIN, SLOUGH's Adjutant, was sent forward in command of the cavalry (O.R. 534) under Capt. WALKER and the pickets ahead. The pickets found SCURRY on the west side of a small gulch just west of the main battlefield (see first position map, Map No. 1) with the Confederate artillery (3 cannons) ON the Santa Fe Trail. A Federal rider was sent back to report to SLOUGH and alert the troops at Pigeon's. The first Confederate cannon shots came through the cottonwoods at Pigeon's while the Federal troops were reforming for the battle.

GLORIETA, FIRST POSITION, DEPLOYMENT
MORNING: 10:00-11:00 AM
FEDERAL DEPLOYMENT:

WALKER dismounted and moved up into woods on the left of the Santa Fe Trail to skirmish on foot, at about which time Capt. RITTER's battery with its infantry support arrived and took position ON the Santa Fe Trail. WALKER then moved up onto a slight elevation in and to the left of the Santa Fe Trail; the Federal battery was still to WALKER's right. WALKER was relieved from this first holding position on the arrival of DOWNING and SOPRIS, at which time SLOUGH ordered WALKER to accompany him (as a mounted escort) for 1/2 to 3/4 hour. At the end of this duty WALKER was assigned to the reserve.

Lt. Col. TAPPAN was assigned command of the Colorado Volunteers and artillery. Upon his arrival, he deployed skirmishers up to the left under DOWNING with Co. D, (up into the pines and probably on the flat where the highway is now located) just west of the high area. From here they moved to advance as the left of the attempted Federal pincers movement.

The Federal left-center included Capt. ROBBINS, Co. K., and the infantry support for the battery of four 12-pound mountain howitzers behind under Lt. CLAFLIN. (This battery was also up in pines, and, per Whitford, "among the trees and within sight of the enemy, who was across the gulch on its west side.")

The right-center included Capt. SOPRIS, Co. C, providing infantry support for the battery of two 12-pound and two 6-pound guns behind under Capt. RITTER on the Santa Fe Trail.

The Federal right consisted of Lt. KERBER (of Capt. MAILIE's Germans) and Lt. BAKER with Co. I. These troops under KERBER/BAKER were across the Santa Fe Trail and north of the small gulch (coming down from the west through the pines between the forces), on across the flat, and across the banks of the arroyo ("ditch"), and up the slope of the ridge on the north of the battlefield.

In the rear, serving as reserves and wagon-train supply protection, were the cavalry and the remaining infantry. The cavalry was under Capt. WALKER and the infantry under Capt. WILDER, Co. G. Walker had been reassigned to the reserve on release from providing escort duty for SLOUGH.

CONFEDERATE DEPLOYMENT:

SCURRY formed a line from the arroyo right "up into the pine forest," the artillery was "ordered to the front on this ridge, and to begin firing immediately on the Federals, advancing rapidly toward the opposite ridge" from Pigeon's, per Whitford.

Again, per Whitford, SCURRY deployed "right...toward the southern end of the ridge he was occupying...middle near the artillery...(left) under himself to the northern end of the ridge and across the old Santa Fe Trail."

SCURRY's deployed line, then, was on the level from within the pines south of the Santa Fe Trail with the Confederate right under Maj. PYRON, the center under Maj. RAGUET extending to the north across the Santa Fe trail to the gulch, and the left directly under SCURRY up to a fence. (This position is just west of where remnants of the Santa Fe Trail can be found crossing up from east along the old highway to continue west.)

The Confederate battery under BRADFORD was on the trail (WALKER reported "three pieces on the trail ready to receive us," O.R.), and then had to move up into the pines west later in order to be the reported Confederate "masked cannon" of the Federal reference in Whitford.

Confederate Artillery LT. BRADFORD was wounded, after which the Confederate force was without an artillery officer. The guns were withdrawn without SCURRY's awareness. He ordered 2 guns brought back up. These probed the Federal second position to determine whether the Federals were behind an adobe wall or behind the ledge of rocks.

GLORIETA, FIRST POSITION, ACTION
MORNING: 10:00-11:00 AM

ACTION:

Artillery fire by both sides was heavy. The Confederate artillery commander, Lt. BRADFORD was wounded, the artillery horses killed, and the gunners withdrew.

The Federal's attacked in separate columns on scurry's right and left, in an apparent tactical pincers movement.

The Federal left under DOWNING attacked on the far left in 2 columns, and were stopped by the Confederate right under PYRON and the "masked cannon" (the furthest right of BRADFORD's three guns). The implication of the "masked cannon" is that DOWNING's attack was sufficiently turned toward the Confederate center that it came within fire of the Confederate artillery in the pines up the slope south from the Santa Fe Trail.

The Federal right under BAKER/KERBER (of MAILIE's Germans) attempted to flank the Confederate left up the arroyo on the north of the Confederate line, until, per Whitford, "at a point nearly opposite the Texan artillery on higher ground to the left." This sudden tactical decision by BAKER to try to capture the Confederate guns indicates he must have advanced to at least slightly behind SCURRY's left flank. SCURRY stopped this attack with heavy hand-to-hand combat. Lt. BAKER was killed leading this action.

DOWNING's failure and KERBER's losses forced the Federals to fall back. Outnumbered by "determined" Confederates, the Federal troops fell back to a more defensible second position at Pigeon's ranch and among the rocks.

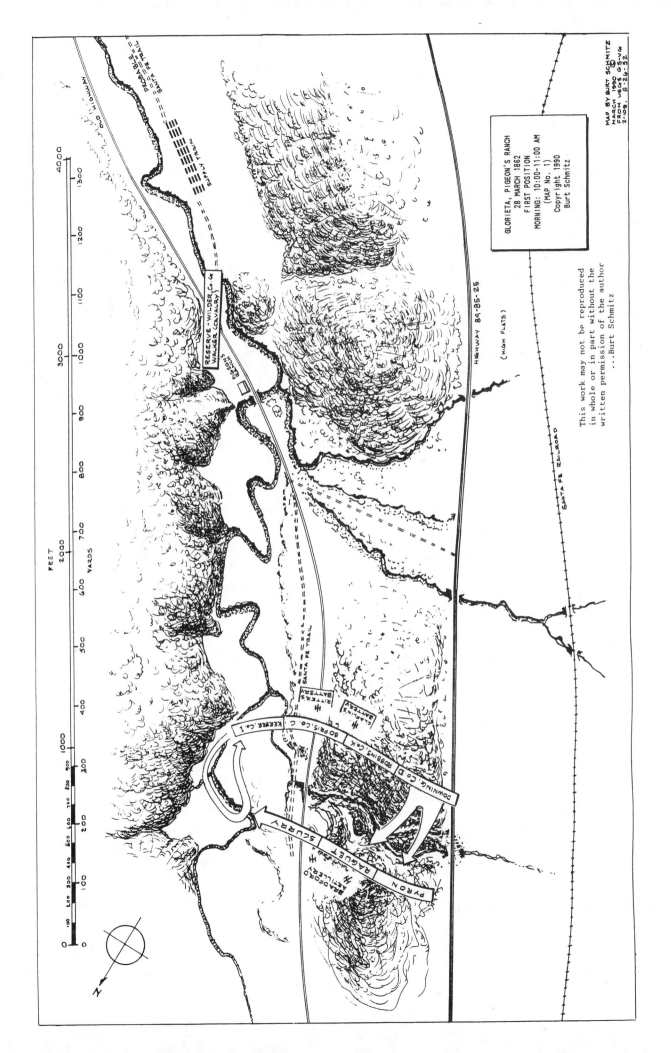

GLORIETA, PIGEON'S RANCH
28 MARCH 1862
FIRST POSITION
MORNING: 10:00-11:00 AM
(MAP No. 1)
Copyright 1990
Burt Schmitz

This work may not be reproduced
in whole or in part without the
written permission of the author
..Burt Schmitz

GLORIETA, PIGEON'S RANCH
28 MARCH 1862
SECOND POSITION
MID-DAY: 11:00 AM-1:00 PM
(MAP NO.2)

FEDERAL DEPLOYMENT:

Lt Col. TAPPAN, in command of the Colorado Vounteers and artillery, fell back to a position "in front of and near Pigeon's house." Per Whitford, they formed in a line along the rough ledge of rocks to the north and below Pigeon's house, across the arroyo near the house, and up on the summit and slope of the wooded rocky bluff to the south. SCURRY describes his tactical uncertainty as to whether Federal troops were stationed behind a "long adobe wall that ran nearly across the canyon or behind a large ledge of rocks in the rear."

KERBER, Co. I, formed the Federal right from the Santa Fe Trail and arroyo up onto the rocks. Company E (40 to 45 enlisted men) of the 3rd Cavalry under WALKER was taken from the reserve, and the first platoon of WILDER were assigned to KERBER (to replace KERBER's heavy losses after the earlier attempt up the arroyo).

SOPRIS, Co. C, and WILDER, Co. G, comprised the Federal center at the foot of the ridge south of the Santa Fe Trail.

CLAFLIN's battery was positioned high up or on top of the ridge (above SOPRIS); his support was Co. K, Capt. ROBBINS. RITTER's battery was positioned partially up the slope from his support, Co. C, SOPRIS and below CLAFLIN. RITTER soon after relocated his battery to the Federal center on the Santa Fe Trail because of exposure to "galling" fire from the Confederate's in their shelter of trees, and because all except one platoon of his supports were assigned to the right and left wings. These were the first platoon of Co. G under WILDER and the 20 men of SOPRIS assigned by TAPPAN. (There is uncertainty to be resolved in the accounts as to whether RITTER relocated after the Confederate battery was disabled about 1:00-2:00 PM, and subsequent anticipation of infantry charges; or, as RITTER implies, the Confederate Artillery was destroyed after his redeployment off the hill and over onto the Santa Fe Trail.)

DOWNING was deployed on the Federal left along the high rocky ridge.

It became apparent to TAPPAN that the Confederates could make a flanking "end run" on the flats to the south and east (along the present highway) around the ridge, get in behind the Federal position and destroy the wagon train. He assigned skirmishers to extend his line far up the flat slope westerly to prevent such a Confederate tactic. This line extended across the present major highway and up at least to the present railroad, with the extreme outer left pickets probably on beyond that. For this, TAPPAN took 20 men from SOPRIS and put them in position on the hill. He felt this was insufficient, so also took the 70 men of Co.F of the unassigned police guard (Capt. COOK had been wounded and Lt. MARSHALL killed at Apache Canyon) and positioned himself with "them in front of and to the left of the batteries on the summit of the hill."

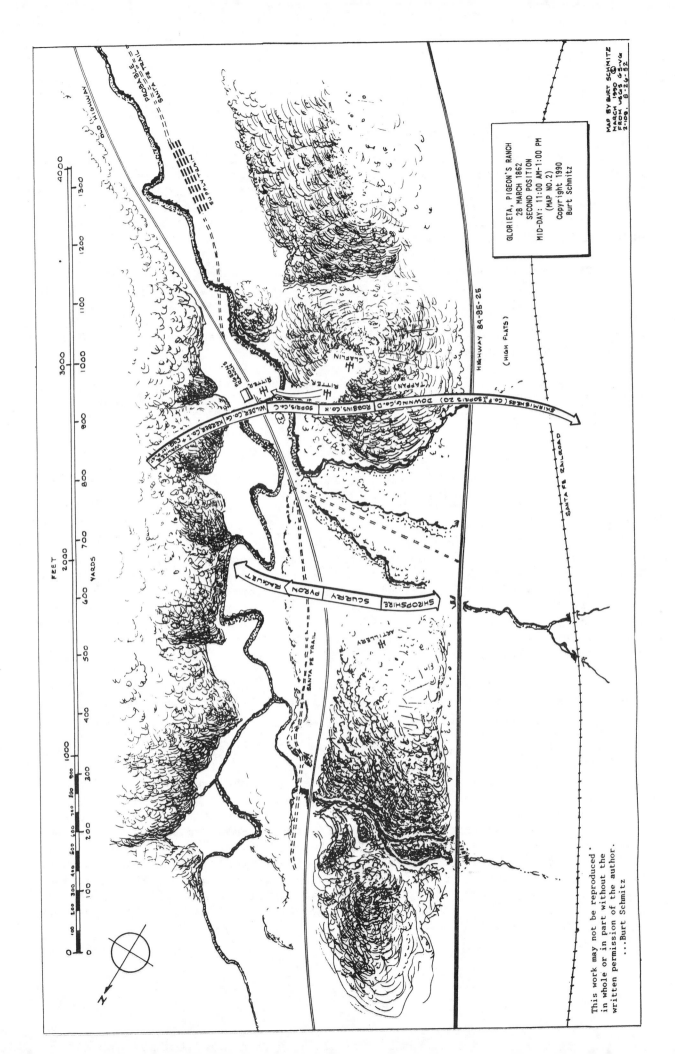

GLORIETA, PIGEON'S RANCH
28 MARCH 1862
SECOND POSITION
MID-DAY: 11:00 AM-1:00 PM
(MAP NO.2)
Copyright 1990
Burt Schmitz

MAP BY BURT SCHMITZ
MARCH 1990
FROM USGS G5va
7-104, 8-26-52

The reserves and cavalry were held in and behind Pigeon's ranch buildings on the north side of the Santa Fe Trail.

CONFEDERATE DEPLOYMENT:

SCURRY advanced 1/4 mile easterly across the ridge (that had been occupied by the Federal troops in the previous first clash) onto the flat slope behind that descended toward Pigeon's Ranch. From here he was at the most 1/4 mile from the reformed second position Federal line (now east of the flat and at the ridge at Pigeon's Ranch, which ridge narrows and closes down the open area of the main battle field into a canyon).

SCURRY deployed Maj. RAGUET to the extreme Confederate left across the arroyo, with Maj. PYRON (now redeployed from the right), to press the Federal troops on the north ridge. PYRON's position was the Confederate left-center from the Santa Fe Trail left to the arroyo. SCURRY held the Confederate right-center from the trail to the south up the slope, and assigned SHROPSHIRE on the Confederate extreme right.

The Confederate artillery was positioned on the right up the slope behind the SCURRY/SHROPSHIRE right. After the wounding of BRADFORD and because of a shortage of gunners, the artillery now consisted of only 2 of the 3 guns. The guns were manned by Pvt. KIRK of PHILLIPS' and Sgt. PATRICK.

GLORIETA, SECOND POSITION, ACTION
MID-DAY: 11:00 AM-1:00 PM

ACTION:

An artillery duel between the opposing batteries ensued, resulting in the destruction of the Confederate artillery, probably about 1:00 PM. It was during this period TAPPAN realized the necessity for deployment of skirmishers out to the Federal left. (These were effective for "4 hours" in blocking a number of probes by SCURRY.) SCURRY's initial problem was determining the well covered position of the Federal troops, and most of his initial action was probing for that purpose.

RITTER's Federal battery was subjected to "galling" fire by the Confederates in his exposed position on the slope of the south ridge in the cover of the pines. (There is the possibility that this "galling" fire was that of a lone Confederate soldier who, because of the similarity of uniforms, had successfully infiltrated undetected behind the Federal line during a later skirmish.) Upon the removal and reassigment of his supports, SOPRIS and WILDER (except 1 platoon), RITTER relocated from the foot of the hill to the Santa Fe Trail. While in this position, the Confederate battery was disabled. (If this is accurate in the records, RITTER moved before the Confederate artillery was destroyed; implying TAPPAN took SOPRIS and extended his wings while the Confederate artillery was still functional).

It appears that much of this redeployment (ending the initial 11:00 AM position and action, and beginning the next phase, the 1:00 PM deployment) resulted at about the time the Confederate artillery was destroyed, perhaps overlapping, in that SOPRIS's redeployment came first and the battery destruction followed.

GLORIETA, PIGEON'S RANCH
28 MARCH 1862
SECOND POSITION
EARLY AFTERNOON: 1:00-2:00 PM
(MAP NO.3)

FEDERAL DEPLOYMENT:

The Federal deployment remained essentially as established in a defensive position along the high front of the ridges and at Pigeon's Ranch buildings as redeployed after the fall back at about 11:00 AM (upon the shock of discovering that, for all their spirit, the Colorado Volunteers and Federal regulars were not the ones on the offensive).

The Federal left, under the important direct attention of Lt. Col. TAPPAN in command of the Colorado Volunteers and batteries, had been reinforced and extended out south up to the present day railroad by Capt. DOWNING, Co. D, with 20 additional pickets drawn from SOPRIS and Lt. WILSON, Co. F, (reassigned from duty as police guard). The center under WILDER and SOPRIS were also under TAPPAN's direction.

The Federal right, from the arroyo up onto the ridge consisted of Lt. KERBER, Co. I, reinforced by Capt. WALKER with the dismounted cavalry from the reserve and the first platoon of WILDER.

The split off and reassignment to both Federal wings of some of the WILDER and SOPRIS supports for RITTER's Battery had caused him to relocate from the base of the hill to the Santa Fe Trail "nearly in front of the ranch." His supports, per Whitford, were still SOPRIS, Co. C, joined by WILDER, Co. G. Before and upon the destruction of the two Confederate guns by RITTER's battery in this position on the Santa Fe Trail by gunner Pvt. KELLY, Co. E, Fifth Infantry, revisions of the deployment were made to meet an expected change of tactics by the Confederates to infantry charges.

At some point RITTER's battery was ordered by Capt. CHAPIN (O.R. 540) from its position on the Santa Fe Trail in front of Pigeon's to "cross the ravine to the other side of the canyon." Lt. CLAFLIN's battery of mountain howitzers with his support, ROBBINS, was ordered down off the hill to join RITTER in this position. From here they could sweep the road ahead toward the Confederates.

CONFEDERATE DEPLOYMENT:

Upon the disabling of the Confederate battery, Col. SCURRY was forced to change to infantry attacks to break the Federal line. SCURRY was reinforced by 125 WAGON TRAIN guards (two companies) from the Confederate supply train at Canyoncito. SCURRY deployed Maj's. RAGUET and PYRON to left, Maj. SHROPSHIRE with Capt. SHANNON to the right, while he commanded the center. His initial deployment problem was need to determine the location of the Federal line, for which he planned a series of infantry probes.

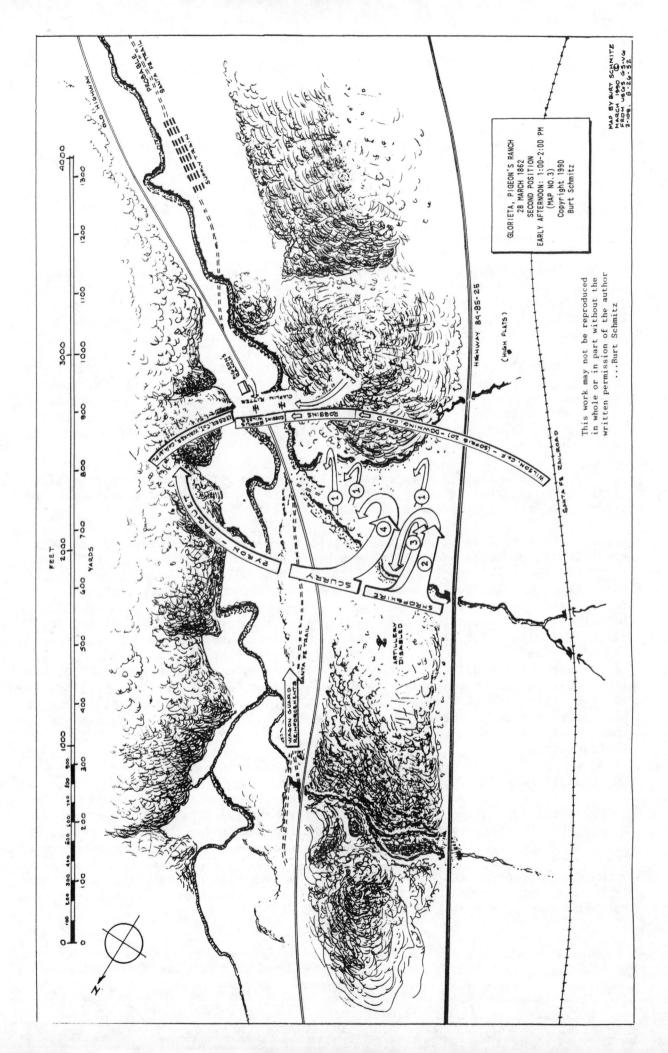

GLORIETA, PIGEON'S RANCH
28 MARCH 1862
SECOND POSITION
EARLY AFTERNOON: 1:00-2:00 PM
(MAP NO. 3)
Copyright 1990
Burt Schmitz

This work may not be reproduced
in whole or in part without the
written permission of the author
...Burt Schmitz

MAP BY BURT SCHMITZ
MARCH 1990
FROM USGS G5-Va
2-109. 8-26-52

GLORIETA, SECOND POSITION, ACTION
EARLY AFTERNOON: 1:00-2:00 PM

SCURRY made the first (1) of several Confederate probing forays with small squads at various unidentified points to determine the location of the Federal line. The intention was that these would draw fire, thus allowing SCURRY to observe and place the Federal's blue smoke.

From his position, TAPPAN had a view of the whole valley. He noted 200-300 Confederates forming up for an attack and reported this to SLOUGH. Soon after, he was informed by SLOUGH of the Confederate plan to take the Federal left from which the Confederates could assault the batteries and the 100 wagons of the supply train.

One half hour later, men in the "same uniforms as the Colorado Volunteers" approached the left Federal line. (This similarity of uniforms was not unusual. These were undoubtedly militia uniforms acquired from the Federal Texas forts at the outbreak of the Civil War; the dark blue coat and light blue trousers were the standard army uniform over the whole of the U.S.) These men requested the Federals not to shoot, claiming to be Federals. They were allowed to come close because SLOUGH's morning plan had been for CHIVINGTON to assault the Confederate rear, which was expected to occur at any time, and it was thought these might be CHIVINGTON's men. Upon determination these were Confederates, the Federals opened fire.

The next attack came again on the Federal left, at (2) under Maj. SHROPSHIRE at the head of a battalion from the Confederate right. SHROPSHIRE was killed, and Capt. SHANNON taken prisoner. (Per TAPPAN, O.R. 537, this occurred "at the time the enemy charged our battery.")

The third (3) was led by SCURRY at the same place from the Confederate right, and was again repulsed by the Federal skirmishers.

SCURRY made a fourth (4) charge from the Confederate right center between the Santa Fe Trail and to the left of the attempt by both SHROPSHIRE (2) and his own (3) at the same place. He was again repulsed by TAPPAN's Federal left which shifted its attention slightly to its right to meet this charge. SCURRY gave up any further attempts for a major assault from his right, though periodic probes were sent this way.

RAGUET and PYRON moved to the Confederate left and up on to the ridge against the Federal KERBER, reinforced by WALKER, and the first platoon from WILDER, gradually pushing them back in close hand to hand fighting, "rock to rock and tree to tree."

CLAFLIN's battery was moved down onto the Santa Fe Trail from the high rocks to join with RITTER who had "crossed the ravine and to the other side of the canyon" to cover the center against SCURRY's charges and the ridge to the north against RAGUET and PYRON.

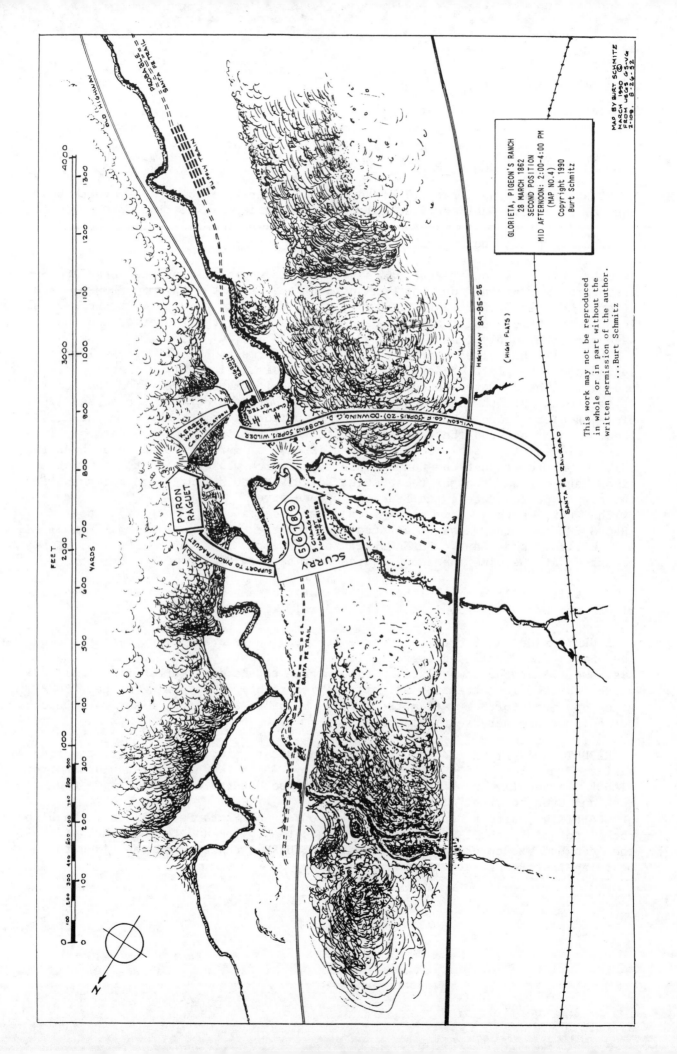

GLORIETA, PIGEON'S RANCH
28 MARCH 1862
SECOND POSITION
MID AFTERNOON: 2:00-4:00 PM
(MAP NO.4)
Copyright 1990
Burt Schmitz

This work may not be reproduced in whole or in part without the written permission of the author. ...Burt Schmitz

MAP BY BURT SCHMITZ
MARCH 1990
FROM UCG-22 GSVG
2-109, 8-26-52

GLORIETA, PIGEON'S RANCH
28 MARCH 1862
SECOND POSITION
MID AFTERNOON: 2:00-4:00 PM
(MAP NO.4)

FEDERAL DEPLOYMENT:

RITTER and CLAFLIN's batteries with their supports, SOPRIS, WILDER, and ROBBINS, were placed just in front of the crossing of the Santa Fe Trail and arroyo. Here they commanded the Confederate approach on the Santa Fe Trail as well as RAGUET and PYRON's advancing position on the ridge to the Federal right.

The Federal troops under KERBER, Co. I, with WALKER's dismounted cavalry and the first platoon of WILDER were confronting the Confederate advance of RAGUET and PYRON on the rocky north edge of the canyon.

On the Federal left and center, Lt. Col. Tappan remained in command of the Colorado Volunteers and batteries. His line from the batteries in the road, with their supports of SOPRIS, WILDER, and ROBBINS, extended south along the ridge under DOWNING, Co. D with the 20 men from SOPRIS, and Lt. WILSON, Co. F. As the Confederates advanced on the ridge to the Federal right, TAPPAN began to draw in these outlying troops to prevent being cut off from the Federal center body at Pigeon's Ranch.

The Federal center consisted for the most part of the battery supports and DOWNING and came to include the above as SCURRY shifted his weight to the Confederate left.

CONFEDERATE DEPLOYMENT:

SCURRY, commanding the Confederate center and right, noted the successful advance of the Confederate left under RAGUET and PYRON against the Federal troops on top of the ridge. With that, he essentially gave up his center and right, shifting the main forces from there to unite on the left with this decisive advance on the ridge and to his own position 300 yards west of Pigeon's Ranch house on the Santa Fe Trail to increase the force of his attack on the Federal batteries.

GLORIETA, SECOND POSITION, ACTION
MID AFTERNOON: 2:00-4:00 PM

While RAGUET and PYRON were successfully pushing the Federals back on SCURRY's left, advancing on top of the ridge, SCURRY charged down down the Santa Fe Trail against the combined battery 5 times (5,6,7,8,9) to try to capture the Federal batteries and drive the Federal skirmishers from top of the ledges, but without success.

RAGUET was killed up on the ridge, after which the drive by the Confederate troops on this ridge continued under PYRON. The Federal troops under KERBER, with WALKER and the first platoon from WILDER, were driven back until the Confederates had possession of the ridge directly above and commanding the Federal batteries. RITTER had one of his artillerymen killed, two wounded, and two of his artillery horses killed, upon which the Federal battery immediately abandoned its untenable position below on the Santa Fe Trail.

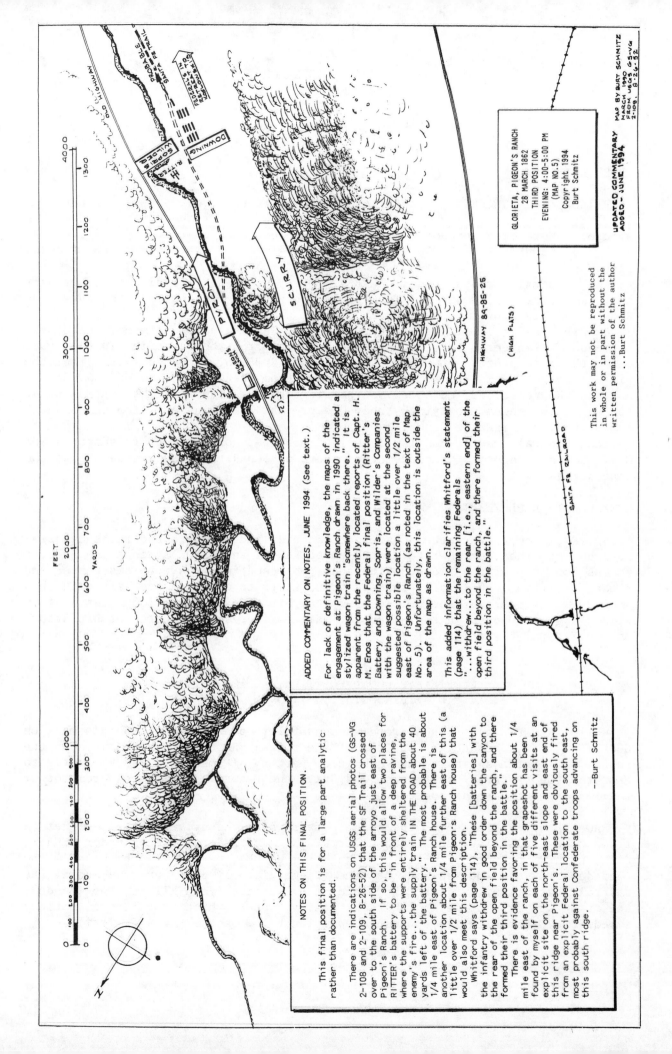

NOTES ON THIS FINAL POSITION.

This final position is for a large part analytic rather than documented.

There are indications on USGS aerial photos (GS-VG 2-108 and 2-109, 8-26-52) that the SF Trail crossed over to the south side of the arroyo just east of Pigeon's Ranch. If so, this would allow two places for RITTER's battery to be "in front of a deep ravine, where the supports were entirely sheltered from the enemy's fire...the supply train IN THE ROAD about 40 yards left of the battery." The most probable is about 1/4 mile east of Pigeon's Ranch house. There is another location about 1/4 mile further east of this (a little over 1/2 mile from Pigeon's Ranch house) that would also meet this description.

Whitford says (page 114), "These [batteries] with the infantry withdrew in good order down the canyon to the rear of the open field beyond the ranch, and there formed their third position in the battle."

There is evidence favoring the position about 1/4 mile east of the ranch, in that grapeshot has been found by myself on each of five different visits at an explicit site on the north-east slope and east end of this ridge near Pigeon's. These were obviously fired from an explicit Federal location to the south east, most probably against Confederate troops advancing on this south ridge.

--Burt Schmitz

ADDED COMMENTARY ON NOTES, JUNE 1994 (See text.)

For lack of definitive knowledge, the maps of the engagement at Pigeon's Ranch drawn in 1990 indicated a stylized wagon train "somewhere back there." It is apparent from the recently located reports of Capt. H. M. Enos that the Federal final position (Ritter's Battery and Downing, Sopris, and Wilder's Companies with the wagon train) were located at the second suggested possible location a little over 1/2 mile east of Pigeon's Ranch (as noted in the text of Map No. 5). Unfortunately, this location is outside the area of the map as drawn.

This added information clarifies Whitford's statement (page 114) that the remaining Federals "...withdrew...to the rear [i.e., eastern end] of the open field beyond the ranch, and there formed their third position in the battle."

GLORIETA, PIGEON'S RANCH
28 MARCH 1862
THIRD POSITION
EVENING: 4:00-5:00 PM
(MAP NO.5)
Copyright 1994
Burt Schmitz

UPDATED COMMENTARY
ADDED - JUNE 1994

MAP BY BURT SCHMITZ
MARCH 1990
FROM USGS GS-VG
2-109, 8-26-52

PROBABLE NEW SANTA FE TRAIL
FEDERALS DISMOUNTED
OLD HIGHWAY
SOPRIS
WILDER
RITTER
DOWNING
PYRON
SCURRY
PIGEON'S
HIGHWAY 84-85-26
(HIGH FLATS)
SANTA FE RAILROAD

FEET
YARDS

GLORIETA, THIRD POSITION, DEPLOYMENT AND ACTION
28 MARCH 1862
EVENING: 4:00-5:00 PM
(MAP NO.5)

CONFEDERATE POSITION:

LEFT; Maj. PYRON.
CENTER and RIGHT; Lt. Col. SCURRY.

FEDERAL POSITION:

Col. SLOUGH ordered the Federal troops to fall back to Koslowski's at 5:00 PM, but the orders did not reach RITTER, nor apparently TAPPAN, who upon seeing the hazard of remaining in his cut off position on the former Federal left, "ordered his men to fall in on the rear of the retiring column." DOWNING was the last to leave the bluff at Pigeon's, and he and RITTER's battery were the last to leave the field at Pigeon's.

RITTER's battery fell back from possibly 1/4 mile to a little over 1/2 mile from Pigeon's Ranch house to the "rear of the open field beyond the ranch." His position in front of a deep ravine was selected by Capt. CHAPIN; his supports were entirely sheltered in the ravine. The supply train was "on the Santa Fe Trail 40 yards from the left of the battery."

DOWNING formed the rearguard, and with RITTER's battery "double shotted" delayed the continuing Confederate attack by SCURRY down the center on the Santa Fe Trail, and up on the rocks on both flanks. It is most probable that PYRON continued along the ridge on the north and SCURRY down the Santa Fe Trail and along the ridge on the south, though this was not reported.

The Confederates attempted one last charge against the Federal defense and battery at this last location, but were repelled with great loss and in disorder.

AUTHORS NOTES ON THIS FINAL POSITION: Updated with new information June 1994.

The discovery of the reports of Asst. Q.M. Capt. H. M. Enos has clarified the location and movements of the Federal wagon train during the battle at Pigeon's Ranch on the 28th. (For the full text of these letters, see the Santa Fe Trail Assn. Quarterly, Wagon Tracks, Vol. 8, No. 3, May 1994; SFTA, P.O. Box 31, Woodston, KS 67675. These reports are interesting reading in that they underscore the dangerously injudicious and brash command performance displayed by the political Col. Slough.)

For lack of definitive knowledge, the maps of the engagement at Pigeon's Ranch drawn in 1990 indicated a stylized wagon train "somewhere back there." It is apparent from the reports that the Federal final position (Ritter's Battery and Downing, Sopris, and Wilder's Companies with the wagon train) were located at the second suggested possible location a little over 1/2 mile east of Pigeon's Ranch (as noted in the text of Map No. 5). Unfortunately, this location is outside the area of the map as drawn.

This added information clarifies Whitford's statement (page 114) that the remaining Federals "...withdrew...to the rear [i.e., eastern end] of the open field beyond the ranch, and there formed their third position in the battle."

...Burt Schmitz
June 1994

GLORIETA, CANYONCITO
CONFEDERATE WAGON TRAIN
28 MARCH 1862
AFTERNOON: 1:30-6:00 PM
(MAP .No. 6)

ORDER OF BATTLE (more or less):

FEDERAL:

Maj. CHIVINGTON.
    Regular Army; 1st Battalion, Capt. LEWIS, 60 men.
        5th Inf., Co. A, Lt. BARR, _____ men.
        5th Inf., Co. G, Lt. NORVELL, _____ men.

    1st Regt. Colo. Vol.:
        Capt. LOGAN; Co. B, Lt. JACOBS, 78 men.
        Capt. WYNKOOP; Co. A, Lt. SHAFFER, 68 men.
        Capt. ANTHONY; Co. E, Lt. Lt. DAWSON, 71 men.
        Capt. SANBORN; Co. H, Lt. SANFORD, 80 men.
    2nd Regt. Colo. Vol.:
        Capt. FORD; Independent Co., Lt. DEFORREST. ____ men.

Total = 357 + unknown number (73?) in 3 companies noted above.
Col. SLOUGH's report; 430 men were assigned to CHIVINGTON.

CONFEDERATE WAGON TRAIN AND GUARD:

    Confederate wagons destroyed: CHIVINGTON reported 80; Whitford, 73;
Confederate letter, 85.

    Confederate soldiers at Canyoncito: CHIVINGTON reported 200; Whitford, 250.

    Scurry had sent the supply train forward from Galisteo under Lt. TAYLOR,
7th Regt. with a guard of 100 on the 26th. These were probably still the
assigned guard on the 28th.
    Two companies of the guard had disobeyed orders and run off up the Apache
Canyon to join the action under SCURRY at Pigeon's, arriving in midafternoon.

ACTION:

    CHIVINGTON's force split off from SLOUGH south onto the Galisteo Road at
9:30 AM. After several miles they turned west on the mountains toward
Canyoncito. Upon hearing the sound of .the battle later in the morning,
CHIVINGTON sent a mounted company toward Pigeon's to alert him to any
Confederate force that might come from the rear. The Federal force arrived on
the high point of the mountain overlooking Johnson's Ranch about 1:30 or 2:00
PM. There a Confederate sentinel on the peak was captured.

    Another hour was spent observing and planning. Johnson's Ranch house was
just north of the Santa Fe Trail where it exits the Apache Canyon at
Canyoncito by the church, and the near buildings (adobe) were just on the
south by the trail; the "wagons and draft animals were in a group at the

24

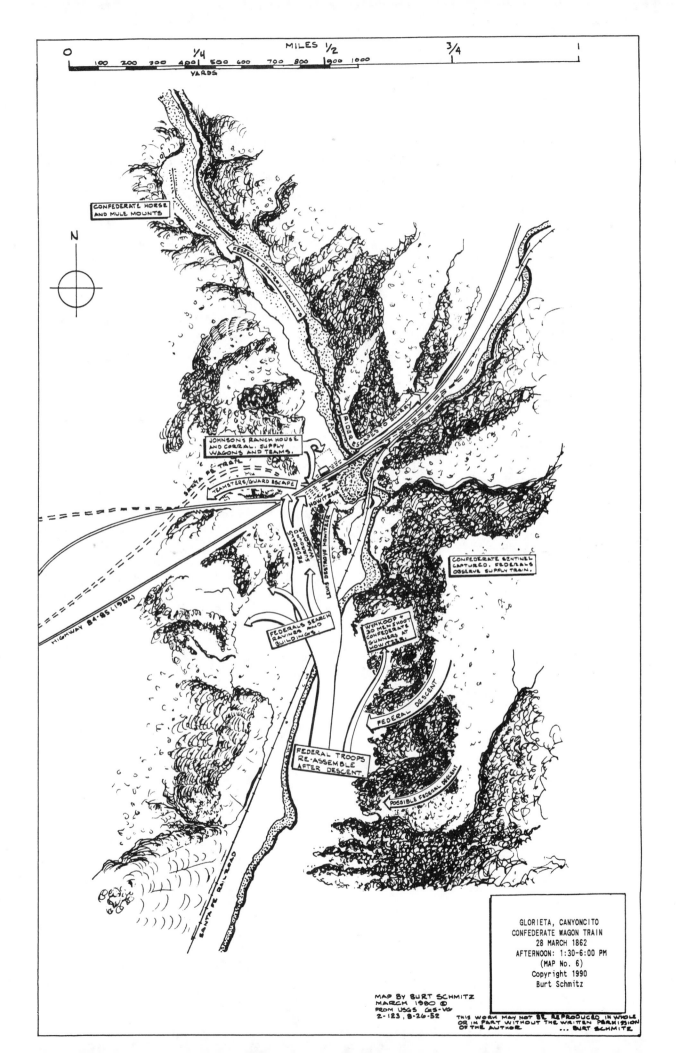

MILES ½

0   ¼   ½   ¾   1

100 200 300 400 500 600 700 800 900 1000
YARDS

N

CONFEDERATE HORSE
AND MULE MOUNTS

FEDERALS DESTROY MOUNTS

IDLER ESCAPES TO CURRY

JOHNSON'S RANCH HOUSE
AND CORRAL. SUPPLY
WAGONS AND TEAMS.

SANTA FE TRAIL

TEAMSTERS/GUARD ESCAPE

HOWITZER

FEDERALS DESTROY HOWITZER

LEWIS DESTROYS HOWITZER

CONFEDERATE SENTINEL
CAPTURED. FEDERALS
OBSERVE SUPPLY TRAIN.

G

HIGHWAY 84-85 (1952)

FEDERALS SEARCH
RAVINES AND
BUILDINGS.

WYNKOOP &
20 MEN SHOOT
CONFEDERATE
GUNNERS AT
MOWITZER.

FEDERAL DESCENT

FEDERAL TROOPS
RE-ASSEMBLE
AFTER DESCENT.

POSSIBLE FEDERAL DESCENT

SANTA FE RAILROAD

GLORIETA, CANYONCITO
CONFEDERATE WAGON TRAIN
28 MARCH 1862
AFTERNOON: 1:30-6:00 PM
(MAP No. 6)
Copyright 1990
Burt Schmitz

MAP BY BURT SCHMITZ
MARCH 1980 ©
FROM USGS G5-VQ
2-123, B-26-52

THIS WORK MAY NOT BE REPRODUCED IN WHOLE
OR IN PART WITHOUT THE WRITTEN PERMISSION
OF THE AUTHOR   ... BURT SCHMITZ

center" (in and near the ranch corral). "Ravines" run to the north and south from this canyon exit. The Confederate howitzer was on the highest of "abrupt" knolls just south of the Santa Fe Trail where it looked directly east into the narrow Apache Canyon trail exit. (More than 100 feet of the north end of this knoll has been lost to the construction of the 4 lane interstate highway circa 1960.) Five to six hundred riding animals (horses and mules) were later found corraled in an arm of a "deep ravine 1/2 mile" away; whether visible from the top of the mountain or not is undetermined, though the implication is they were not.

When ready, the quick Federal descent was ordered. Men were "lowered at first by ropes and straps" over the cliffy steepness at the top. Whitford's description of the initial lowering by ropes places descent 1/4 to 1/2 mile south of the Santa Fe Trail exit. However, at 3/4 mile south descent is also possible down a long, deep gulch.

On hearing the racket of the descending Federals, some of teamsters and infantrymen guards grabbed the horses and mules at hand and escaped down the Santa Fe Trail toward Santa Fe, and several harmless shots were fired from the Confederate howitzer.

At the bottom, the Federal troops quickly reassembled. CHIVINGTON arranged them in "order of battle where they marched and countermarched," still not certain if a large body of Confederates might be in the vicinity.

WYNKOOP and 30 men were deployed on the mountainside to pick off the Confederate gunners on the knoll. The Federals searched the buildings and ravines for Confederates while advancing rapidly north on the train at Johnson's Ranch. Capt. LEWIS was sent up the right to capture and destroy the howitzer on the knoll. The other column attacked and surrounded the wagon train, and began the destruction of the 70 to 80 supply wagons. During this destruction, a lone Confederate on a horse came from the ravine (most probably from the north) and rode away up the canyon east to warn SCURRY at Pigeon's Ranch. It may have been this that alerted the Federals to the additional presence of the 500-600 riding animals (horses and mules) corraled in an "arm of a deep ravine 1/2 mile away." These were bayonneted.

Near dark (6:00 PM) the force again reached the top of the mountain to return by the same route. There, Lt. COBB from SLOUGH met them with an order to return to support the main column. They rejoined the main Federal troops at Kozlowski's about 10:00 PM.